USER-FRIENDLY

PROPHECY

**Insights and Guidelines for the
Effective Use of Spiritual Gifts**

BY

LARRY RANDOLPH

All Scriptures, unless otherwise noted are King James Version.

Copyright (c) 1995 by Larry Randolph.

No part of this book may be reproduced in any form, by mimeograph or any other means, without permission, in writing, from the publisher.

Published by

Cherith Publications
1925 Century Park East #2130
Century City, CA 90067
(800) 555-1359

Printed in the United States of America

First Printing, June 1995

ACKNOWLEDGMENTS

I would like to gratefully acknowledge my friend, Brian Bumpas, for his contribution to this book. Several years ago, while accompanying me on a ministry trip to Scotland, he began to encourage me to commit both my experiences and my knowledge of prophecy to writing. After returning, I spent the rest of that year writing and rewriting this book while lying on the floor of my home office.

After finishing, Brian and I began to co-labor in the lengthy and laborious task of revising the manuscript. In the places where it was necessary to clarify my thoughts, Brian reminded me of one more example that I could use to better make my point. When I was unsure of how to make a particular point, he pulled it out of me with hard questions and sheer determination. Together, we rethought the contents of the book and at times, we fought like cats and dogs over one word. He didn't always win, but in many instances, I was challenged to say things differently or to not say them at all. Thank you Brian, for the many hours you spent with me in the crafting of this book. Thanks for believing in me and, most of all, thanks for being my friend. Without your encouragement and labor of love, I would not have created this book. For this, I am most grateful.

Further Acknowledgments

I want to thank my friend Jean Bernal, who was kind enough to edit the manuscript in its final stages. Thank you for your professionalism, for your suggestions and for your comments. Your labor of love and support was greatly appreciated and needed. Again, thank you for the many hours spent dotting the I's and crossing the T's.

Thanks also goes to two special friends—David Shirk and Fritz Matthews. Thank you Dave, for taking the time to read the entire manuscript. The suggestions you made were invaluable to the completion of this book. Thank you Fritz, for your input, it was greatly appreciated.

I would also like to thank Hal Sparks, Greg Hanks and Joyce Smeltzer for their care, concern and comments at the early stages of this project. Their time, efforts, observations and guidance were appreciated.

DEDICATION

This book is gratefully dedicated to all the members of my family, especially Rebecca, my wife, who has always encouraged me to reach my potential in Christ. Her dedication and love for God and His Word have always been an inspiration to me, whether in everyday life, in the pulpit, or in the writing of this book. She is one of the most prophetic women I have ever known. I love her very much.

James, my father, has also played a vital role in my spiritual life. In addition to fathering me, he has taught me to desire and respect spiritual gifts by modeling them in front of me. Geraldine, my mother, has also been a wonderful example of a Christian who is laden with the fruits of the Spirit. By example, she has taught me to love unconditionally, to be patient, gentle, forgiving, kind, and long-suffering.

Chris, Stephanie, Rene, Roland, and Jonathan, my five children, have also encouraged me in a way they may not know. Their understanding and acceptance of my calling has released me to travel throughout the Body of Christ, where I have birthed many of the principles presented in this book.

Also, thanks to my mother-in-law, Aurora, for all her prayers and support for me.

Publisher's Note

Imagine, if you will, experiencing the life changing power of God speaking words of life and love through and *to* you. That is the essence of the prophetic. The purpose of this book is to release and impart the life changing power of the prophetic to You! The initial impetus for writing this book came out of a series of meetings conducted in Fort Worth, Texas.

In a very simple and easy to understand way, Larry humbly conveyed the essence of this book to those gathered at these meetings. Then he began to demonstrate his message by ministering in power and with authority. I knew many of the people in attendance and I observed with tears of joy and gladness as Larry accurately and precisely exercised his prophetic gift with precision, gentleness and the loving sensitivity of a caring father.

At the conclusion of one of these meetings on a stormy night in April, 1993, I watched as a dear friend of mine, John Smeltzer, came up to Larry and said, "I have been deeply touched by your ministry tonight. I had never realized that the purpose of the prophetic was to encourage and that it was available to all believers. You have changed my life forever. I will never forget what you have taught me tonight nor will I ever view Joyce in the same manner again."

I was seated next to John and Joyce Smeltzer that night and had witnessed how Larry's prophetic words over Joyce had affirmed and uplifted her spirit. John's statement to Larry that night had life changing impact upon my life. It was as though a light had gone off inside me and I heard myself thinking *"this message has to get out, we've got to write a book on this and let people know that the purpose of the prophetic is to encourage and to exhort, to lift up and to edify the Body of Christ and that all believers can receive and use the gift of prophecy."*

As a result, I dedicated myself to persuade Larry to write this book so that people just like you and me could passionately embrace the fact that the prophetic is a gift which God wants each and every one of us to benefit from and bless others with.

For the past two years I have had the unique and wonderful opportunity to travel with Larry and I have witnessed the impact which his ministry has had upon thousands of people. I have worked in close quarters with Larry and have been amazed at his grasp of Scripture and his passionate pursuit of Jesus and the things of God. Many have witnessed and commented upon his humility. Few have seen the ferocity, the strength and the courage with which he has pursued Christ, forsaking all. His pursuit of God has deposited in the depths of his being an intense burning, non-judgmental, passionate love for those who have been created in the image of God—*us*.

The beauty of this book and the essence of Larry's ministry is that Larry has been able to reduce the seemingly complex and mysterious issues surrounding the prophetic into a simple and understandable form. Larry's passionate pursuit of Jesus has heightened his ability to perceive and express the heart of God. Hence, he is able to make the prophetic truly <u>User-Friendly.</u>

Who would benefit from this book? As mentioned, it's been geared towards reducing the mysteries of the prophetic into an understandable form. It will encourage those who, like myself, had never considered themselves capable of operating in the prophetic. If you fit into that category, I guarantee that if you read the book and apply its principles your life will be changed and you will **never** feel unspiritual again! You will find this book to be a frank and open discussion of Larry's life written with the sole purpose of bringing down the barriers which exist between layman and laity, and those that exist between the church and humanity. *Therefore,* I cannot think of one person whom this book would not benefit.

By the way, for those of you who may be Christian scholars or theologians, or for those of you who are active in Christian leadership, I would also like to encourage you to pick up a copy of this book. It may assist you in bringing order to the chaotic and undisciplined characteristics of the prophetic people within your church. I might add that the theologians who scrutinized this book enjoyed reading it and wrote us that they would buy several copies themselves!

In summary, I guess that you have gathered by now that I am rather enthusiastic about this book. Well, you are absolutely right! You see, I am a salesman. The only problem is, I can only sell what I absolutely believe and that which I have faith and confidence in. And since the testimony of Jesus is the Spirit of Prophecy, and since this is the best book I have ever read on prophecy, I encourage you to buy a copy of this book for you and for your loved ones.

Brian W. Bumpas
May, 1995

CONTENTS

PART ONE

Highlights the validity of prophecy in scripture and describes its basic function and use within the church.

CHAPTER 1 - *PROPHETIC HERITAGE* 17
1. Prophetic Environment
2. Chicken-Yard Prophecy
3. New York Prophecy
4. Richard

CHAPTER 2 - *THE PROPHETIC IN THE BIBLE* 27
1. Biblical Overview Of Prophecy
2. Emergence Of Old Testament Prophets
3. Classification Of Prophets
4. School Of The Prophets
5. Description Of Various Old Testament Prophets
6. New Testament Prophets
7. Jesus The Prophet
8. Summary

CHAPTER 3 - *THE GIFT OF PROPHECY* 39
1. 1st Corinthians, The Gifts Of The Spirit
2. Prophecy Defined
3. The Resident Gift
4. A Step Beyond
5. Reception vs. Perception
6. Applying The Principle
7. Summary

CHAPTER 4 - *PROPHECY, THE GREATER GIFT* 51
1. Tongues In Context
2. Setting Order
3. Inspiration vs. Information
4. Tongues vs. Prophecy

CHAPTER 5 - *WHO CAN PROPHESY?* 61
   1. Maturity vs. Availability
   2. Male and Female
   3. Women In Ministry
   4. Junias
   5. Balance
   6. Sons and Daughters
   7. Prophetic Daughters
   8. Prophetic Sons
   9. Nurturing The Prophetic In Children

PART TWO

Sets the stage regarding the basic purpose and ownership of prophecy, and examines both how to manage this gift and integrate it into the church.

CHAPTER 6 - *BASIC PROPHETIC* 77
   1. Edification
   2. Exhortation
   3. Comfort
   4. Encouragement vs. Discouragement

CHAPTER 7 - *ADVANCED PROPHETIC* 87
   1. Conviction
   2. Impartation
   3. Direction
   4. To Foretell

CHAPTER 8 - *HOW TO RECEIVE
                  PROPHETIC REVELATION* 99
   1. Visions
   2. Dreams
   3. Intuition / Impressions
   4. Impressions / Perceptions
   5. Inner Voice / Audible Voice
   6. Mental Pictures

CHAPTER 9 - *STEWARDSHIP OVER*
              THE PROPHETIC 113
  1. Giving Out Of Obedience
  2. Starting Simple
  3. Sticking to the Basics
  4. Starting At the Bottom
  5. The Process of Development

CHAPTER 10 - *RELATING TO THE CHURCH* 123
  1. Identifying Valid Prophetic Ministry
  2. Relating To Authority
  3. Prophets And Submission
  4. The Pastor's Role
  5. A Prophet's *Metron*
  6. Out of Your *Metron*
  7. Prophet / Pastor
  8. Concluding Thoughts

PART THREE

Deals with failure and success; mature and immature prophetic ministry; and answers the forty most commonly asked questions regarding the prophetic.

CHAPTER 11 - *PROPHETIC FAILURE* 135
  1. Fear of Failure
  2. Admitting Failure
  3. When Prophecy Fails
  4. Revelation
  5. Interpretation
  6. Application
  7. Conditional Prophecy
  8. Overview of Prophetic Failure

CHAPTER 12 - *PROPHETIC PITFALLS* 149
    1. "Thus Saith The Lord"
    2. King James Vernacular
    3. Screamers
    4. God's Word or Human Disposition?
    5. Marriages and Babies
    6. Money
    7. Prophetic Manipulation
    8. Counterfeits

CHAPTER 13 - *PROPHETIC WEIRDNESS* 165
    1. Weird or Strange?
    2. Bizarre Prophecies
    3. Judging Weird Prophecies
    4. User Friendly Prophetic
    5. User Friendly Principles
    6. Concluding Thoughts

CHAPTER 14 - *PROPHETIC MATURITY* 177
    1. Charisma or Character
    2. Possessing Maturity
    3. Timing
    4. Compassion
    5. Moses, a Mercy Prophet
    6. Final Conclusion

APPENDIX : *FORTY COMMONLY ASKED
QUESTIONS AND ANSWERS* 189

INTRODUCTION

Over the last 20 years I have been asked both complex and simple questions concerning the gift of prophecy. Inquiring Christians have wanted to know such things as—who can prophecy? What value does prophecy hold in the life of a believer? How do Christians know if they are called to a prophetic ministry? In what manner do people receive and develop prophetic gifting? How do prophetic people relate to the Body of Christ and it's leadership? And most importantly, what is the proper use of prophecy in the 20th Century Church?

Over the years, I have been able to satisfy the curiosity of casual seekers by giving brief and simple answers to their questions. For the most part, a great number of these people have taken my instruction to heart and have applied it to their lives and ministries. As a result they seem better equipped to prophecy.

In the Church, however, there has always been a percentage of people who are not content with simple instruction. Many ordinary people have an extra - ordinary desire to understand the inner - workings of spiritual gifting. This is especially true of prophetic people who have an insatiable hunger to know why, how, when, and where to use their gift.

In response to this common cry for deeper understanding, I have often prayed that someone would write a book, addressing the many issues that surround the gift of prophecy and prophetic ministry. I envisioned a book that was simple to read and easy to understand, but also thorough and in depth. This book would be user friendly, honest, filled with personal examples and laced with humor. It would serve as a simple handbook—giving guidance to those who desired a greater insight into prophetic protocol and procedure. It would de-mystify the cloud of pseudo-spirituality that surrounds both prophecy and prophets. Most importantly, this book would bring a measure of credibility to a much needed ministry gift—one that is so often misunderstood by the Church.

For several years I searched desperately for this kind of book. Although I came across a number of wonderful books on prophecy, I was yet to find what I had envisioned. Then, it dawned on me! The book I was looking for was written upon the pages of my own heart. I had been reared in a prophetic environment and had given most of my life to prophetic ministry. So, why not share my own understanding of prophecy? After all, it was a burden that God had specifically given to me.

As a result of much soul searching *"User Friendly Prophecy"* was finally written. By some standards, it may be lacking in eloquence and style. For the most part, however, it is an honest and heartfelt book designed to equip an emerging generation of prophetic people. More specifically, it is written for those believers who desire to edify, exhort, and comfort the Church through the gift of prophecy.

Larry Randolph

PART ONE

Highlights The Validity Of Prophecy In Scripture

And Describes Its

Basic Function And Use Within The Church

Chapter One

PROPHETIC HERITAGE

My father quietly folded the newspaper he was reading and reached for his old blue coat. "Come on, son," he said. "We're going across town to see a car that's for sale." A split-second later, I was on my feet, following like a puppy behind its master. "How much is the car?" I asked with curiosity. "Do you think we can afford it?"

With an all-knowing look that was common to my dad, he turned, smiled at me, and whispered, "The ad doesn't give the price, son, but I happen to know exactly what they are asking for it." Sure enough, when we arrived at the used-car lot, the salesman attempted to sell us the car for just the price my dad had told me.

Dad was right! In fact, Dad seemed to be right about most things. Whether it was the price of cars, a change in the weather, the names of unannounced dinner guests, or the secret sins of his own children, he seemed to have prior knowledge about things that he couldn't have known naturally. Where did Dad get this secret information? Some say he was clairvoyant or a psychic. Neither of these described Dad. Instead, he was a simple, small-town preacher who was sensitive to "the Spirit of God." His accurate impressions did not come from palmistry or fortune-telling, but were rooted in a conviction that God shares secrets with those who are His friends.

The denomination to which we belonged called such phenomena the "Spirit of Prophecy." Others acknowledged Dad's gift as the "word of knowledge," contained in I Cor. 12:8. For the sake of those who struggle with the theology of spiritual gifting, let's just say that Dad was open to prophetic communication from God. Whether it was at church, at home, or at work, he seemed to be tuned into this frequency of spiritual perception at all times.

17

In spite of those within our denomination who believed that God speaks only within the confines of the church sanctuary, Dad exercised his gifting whenever and wherever necessary. He listened constantly for an inner witness which would direct him in the ordinary, everyday matters of life. His simple faith enabled him to cling to the notion that God not only lived in his heart, but also delighted in speaking to his mind. I repeatedly witnessed how it was possible for Dad to receive and speak forth hidden or unknown information. And, once my father received this revelation, he was faithful to deliver it at any time or in any place. Without hesitation, he would declare this revelatory insight to his family, friends, or total strangers.

Prophetic Environment

Growing up in a prophetic environment can be both frightening and unsettling to a young child. Yet, for me, it was neither. It just seemed natural, like the blue sky that hung over my boyhood home in Arkansas. Perhaps the reason I have always felt comfortable with supernatural gifts is due to my exposure to the godly men and women throughout the formative years of my life.

As long as I can remember, the exercise of supernatural gifting seemed to be a way of life for our family. In fact, some of my earliest memories are hearing stories of miraculous events in the living room of our little house. While sitting on Grandpa's knees, I would listen to stories of our Uncle Newton who was a prophetic miracle worker in the early 1900's. With great conviction, Grandpa would recount the many healings worked on those who were blind, deaf, or crippled.

Occasionally, Dad would interrupt and relate how his own life had been spared by a warning in a dream. He would continue with recent examples of healings and visitations within the lives of our family members. Soon, others would join in the excitement of the testimonies and recount how my grandfather was saved from a premature death through the prayers of my father.

18

As the evening wore on, stories of miracles, healings, dreams, visions and prophetic signs evolved into a crescendo of high praise of the Lord. By this time, the atmosphere was so charged with spiritual awareness that I remember feeling overwhelmed by the power of God's presence. I would sit speechless, in awe of a sovereign God who responds to the simple faith of common people.

Chicken-Yard Prophecy

By the time I had entered grade school, I had developed an infatuation with the prophetic. On many nights, I would lay sleepless and ponder the mysteries of the supernatural. Could *I* flow in the gifts of the Spirit? Would God use *me* in the ministry of the miraculous? These were the thoughts of a six-year-old boy, inspired by a spiritual heritage enriched by godly predecessors.

My first chance to test the prophetic gifting in my life came when I was in the first grade. On a cold winter morning, I awakened with a strange impression. I felt drawn to the chicken yard which lay behind our house. It seemed that I instinctively knew how many eggs our hens had laid the night before. I jumped out of bed and ran to the hen house with great expectation. My heart pounded with excitement as I began to search the nests. I counted slowly -- one, two, three, four, five... Right! I leaped with joy, thrilled that I had found the exact number of eggs which earlier I had perceived would be there.

This incident might seem relatively insignificant to those who are spiritually mature; however, in my mind, I had launched out into a journey into the realm of the prophetic. This chicken-yard prophecy was a small beginning, but from that day forward I had a sense that my gifting could later develop into something of use in God's kingdom.

New York Prophecy

The year was 1977. As I stepped off the jumbo jet at La Guardia Airport in New York City, I was deep in thought, reflecting upon the past few decades of my life. More than twenty years had passed since my chicken yard prophecy and my prophetic gifting had grown considerably. Although I no longer knew how many eggs were in the hen house, I was sure that God had placed a prophetic call on my life. I had determined to fulfill that call in a way that would be pleasing to God and beneficial to His people.

As I approached the crowd of unfamiliar faces in the airport terminal, I was perplexed. It seemed hard to believe, but I had just traveled over fifteen hundred miles from my home in Arkansas in blind obedience to a prophetic dream which I had been given. Had I lost my mind? Or was I really operating with the mind of Christ? The implications of what I was doing began to dawn on me. Nevertheless, I was absolutely certain about three things.

First, earlier that month, I had a prophetic dream in which I was instructed to visit New York City. I was given no further information, other than seeing a vision of a white late-model car -- which would later play a significant role in my trip. Second, in spite of the fact that I was broke, scared, and had never ventured out of my home state before, much less flown on a plane, I was determined to obey what I believed to be a prophetic word from the Lord. Third, out of obedience, I was now in a strange city, completely dependent upon God's divine leading and providence.

As I picked up the pay phone to summon a taxi, my mind began racing with all kinds of questions. *This faith and obedience stuff is great*, I thought, *but, now that I am here, what in the world am I going to do?* I didn't know anyone on the East Coast, much less in New York City. I was totally alone, with no place to stay. To complicate matters, I had used all but $100 of my money to pay for the round-trip airline ticket. Even if God multiplied my money

20

threefold, I would neither be able to rent a hotel room nor buy enough food for the three days I was scheduled to be there.

In spite of my concerns, I squared my shoulders and put my best foot forward in faith. I boldly stepped into the awaiting taxi and asked the driver to take me to Stony Brook, Long Island, where I had heard that a Messianic conference was being held. Upon arrival, I randomly selected a hotel and used the remainder of my money to rent a room for the night. Clutching my last few dollars, I stumbled into the hotel cafe to have a cup of coffee and to ponder my strange predicament.

As I sat down, my faith began to waver as old doubts began to surface. *Why would God require such a thing from me anyway?* I mumbled. *Doesn't He care that I have no money to live on, or a way back to the airport? Why am I here anyway? Have I missed God?* I sat still for a moment, awaiting an answer. When none came, I shrugged my shoulders in exasperation and turned to the only source of comfort I had at the moment -- my cup of coffee.

As I began to sip the warm coffee, I felt the Spirit of the Lord descend on me. Without knowing why, my attention was drawn to a man sitting at a table in the back of the restaurant. He was middle-aged, well-dressed, and seemed to be dining alone. At first, it appeared that this gentleman's attention was solely focused upon his food. However, as our eyes met, he seemed to lose interest in everything but our exchange of glances. Every few seconds, he would look up from his table and stare at me, as if he desperately needed something.

What's wrong with this guy? I thought. *What does he want from me? And, why do I feel sorry for him?* He didn't display any obvious signs of trouble or pain. There didn't seem to be anything out of the ordinary about this man other than a rather melancholy expression on his face. Then, for the first time since I had left Arkansas, the Lord began to speak to me. He indicated that the man in the business suit was suicidal and that I was to go sit down beside him.

I was shocked! *No Way Lord! I was willing to brave flying in an airplane for the first time -- even though I've been afraid of heights. I was willing to come to New York without provision, but I'm not going to make a fool out of myself in this restaurant! If You want me to speak to this man, You will have to have him approach me!*

Feeling confident that I was now off the hook, I quickly got into the line at the cash register to pay for my coffee. I had just stuck my change in my pocket when I felt a gentle tap on my right shoulder. At first I thought it was an impatient customer who was urging me to hurry out of the line. But much to my surprise, I heard a voice behind me saying, "Sir, are you a minister?" As I turned to see who had tapped my shoulder, I was dumbfounded. The gentleman whom the Lord had spoken to me about was now standing in front of me with a look of desperation upon his face.

How did he know that I was a minister? I thought. Before that day, I had neither seen nor talked to this man before. *Is this you God? Would you bring me to New York to help one man?* With these thoughts swirling around in my mind, I followed the man back to his table, where he began to tell me about his life.

Richard

His name was Richard. He was raised Catholic, but rarely went to mass. He believed in God; however, until recently, he had seen no reason to commit his life to the Lord. Prior to that year, he had a nice car, a beautiful wife, wonderful kids, and a partnership in a growing company. Everything seemed to be going his way until suddenly his world fell apart.

Approximately eight months before (much to the dismay of those who knew them both), his wife of many years had filed for a divorce. He had been asked to move out of his house and forbidden to speak to his children. To add to this dilemma, his business began to falter. He had seemingly lost all hope and could not find a reason to live.

With great pain in his voice, Richard continued to tell me about the events leading up to our encounter. Two days prior to our meeting, he had left his home in Wisconsin to drive into New York to conduct business. In his mind, it was the last trip he would ever take. Once he had concluded his business, he was determined to kill himself with the gun he had stashed in the glove compartment of his car.

En route to New York, something significant had happened. He had tuned his car radio onto a gospel station where he heard R. W. Shambach preach the message of salvation. For the first time in his life, Richard had decided to pray. "Lord, if You are really there and You care about me, I want to know. Otherwise, I am going to kill myself." At that point, he made an unusual request of the Lord. Almost reluctantly, he murmured, "God, if you will send a minister to talk to me while I'm in New York, I will reconsider my plans." Richard hesitated and then said, "That's why I approached you." He then continued, "I just had a feeling that you were a minister and could possibly help me. Are you the one? Can you really help me?"

As I struggled to control my heightened emotions, I paused briefly to gather my thoughts. Then, in faith, I opened my mouth believing that God would give me the right thing to say. "Sir, I now know why I am in New York. Would you believe that God loves you so much, that He would go to any lengths or extremes to help you? Would you believe that He would move heaven and earth to divinely orchestrate our meeting? Most importantly, would you also believe that our God is so extravagant that He would send an insignificant, small-town, preacher all the way from Arkansas on a blind journey just to say, '*God loves you, please don't take your life?*'"

23

With tears running down his face, Richard reached out and grabbed my hand. Looking directly into my eyes, he said, "What can I do to be saved? Will you come up to my hotel room and tell me more about the love of God?" Without hesitating a moment, I responded "Yes, God wants to save you and to fill you with His Spirit."

Richard immediately responded to these words of hope, and led me to his room where he encountered the Living Lord. After several hours of talking, praying, and shedding tears of repentance, he was gloriously saved, delivered from his despair, and baptized in the Holy Spirit. Apparently, it had taken months for God to orchestrate this meeting, but in a matter of hours a miracle had taken place. Richard's life was forever changed. He had found help in a God who was quick to respond to his cry of desperation.

Now that God had met Richard's needs, my situation was also about to change. I would soon discover that **when God leads -- He provides**. I had been willing for God to use me in Richard's life, and now this new believer had an intense desire to be a channel for my need. Richard felt impressed to buy my meals and pay my hotel bill for the remainder of my stay. In my eyes, it was a miracle of provision. I had been faithful to God and He was now being faithful to me.

When it was time for me to return home, there was yet another blessing in store for me. Richard felt that he should drive me to the airport. When I saw his car, I was stunned. It was the same, late-model white car which I had seen in the prophetic dream I had received. Now I was seated in the front seat, conversing with the man whose prayer in this car had supernaturally interrupted my life and brought me to a place so far from home.

That fall day in 1977 was the last time I laid eyes upon Richard. However, I often think about him and the lessons I learned through that experience. Several thoughts come to mind.

First, I thank God for the value of the prophetic. It is an endowment from God which is essential in accomplishing spiritual ministry. This instance in Richard's life demonstrates that an integral part of God's evangelistic outreach is carried out through prophetic ministry.

Also, I thank God for the grace and strength He gave me to obey His prophetic word. My experience taught me that **it is a great thing to receive a prophetic word, but an even greater act of spiritual maturity to obey that word.** In Richard's case, had I not been obedient to God's prophetic instruction, he might have perished.

Next, I'm thankful for the prophetic heritage which I received simply by being a member of a godly family. I became sensitive to the Spirit through a process in which my parents imparted and cultivated the gifts of the Spirit within their children. I remember with fondness how my father and grandfather encouraged me to memorize and recite scriptures at an early age. Consequently, when I minister in the Church, I find myself in deep appreciation for the spiritual environment in which I was raised, thanking God for my parents, grandparents, aunts, and uncles who first introduced me to the realm of supernatural phenomenon.

Finally, My spiritual heritage fostered a life-long quest to gain biblical insight and understanding of my prophetic purpose and function within the Body of Christ. As a result, I have come to value the written word of God as a living training manual and historical workbook designed to equip and instruct the saints in the development of their prophetic gifts and callings. Therefore, in the next chapter we shall discuss the absolute certainty, usefulness and importance of prophetic gifting in biblical context.

Chapter Two

THE PROPHETIC IN THE BIBLE

Life has shown me that people who are acknowledged as skillful or experts within a specific field initially began by understanding the basics of that skill. This seems to be true of almost any trade, skill, or craft. For example, those who are experienced in the fine arts (dance, drama, musical instruments, etc.) began by understanding the origin, history, and basic function of their craft. They didn't achieve expert status by starting at the top of their trade. Instead, they began at the bottom -- applying simple, basic principles.

This principle also applies to sports. Many acknowledge Jerry Rice as the greatest football receiver of all time. Television analysts, teammates, and coaches consistently point out that the key to his success is that he has drilled himself in the fundamentals of the sport. The patterns he runs and the spectacular plays he makes during a game are merely a reflex -- a conditioned response birthed by practicing the basics.

In the same way, Christians who desire to operate in the prophetic must first familiarize themselves with the fundamental principles of prophecy. Like artists and athletes, we must study the textbook, practice its principles, and play by the rules. As a result, we gain mastery over the skills needed to accomplish prophetic ministry.

Before doing these things, however, there are several questions that must be answered. First, what is the proper textbook for prophecy? Is it the Bible? And, if so, is there validation for the prophetic in both the Old and New Testaments? Second, are we safe in building our prophetic ministry from the fabric of scripture? How can we be sure our prophetic gifts are in line with biblical doctrine? Finally, were men and women of the Bible prophetic in spirit and gifting?

A large part of the answer to these questions can be summed up in one statement: **the Bible is our handbook for prophecy.** Every essential element we need to operate in the prophetic can be found in its pages. Moreover, the revealed word of God documents the role of the prophetic throughout the history of Israel and the early church.

Therefore, like a football player reviews the history of the game by studying the films of those who have played before him, we can learn from the failure and success of the prophetic figures described in the Bible. We can also enhance our own performances through close examination of the methods and techniques which they used to exercise their gifting.

For example, to develop my gift, I have studied the historical context of the times in which the prophets lived to determine how they were influenced by it. I have also examined the influential roles they played in both the church and society. The observations I gained from these studies have proven to be beneficial to my ministry. So, in the following pages of this chapter, we will examine the validity of prophecy, its impact, and its function as seen in the lives of biblical characters.

Biblical Overview of Prophecy

Several years ago I heard a pastor say, "I don't want the gift of prophecy operating in my church. I just want to stick to Jesus and sound Bible doctrine." To some, this pastor's opinion might appear to be wise or, at least, worthy of consideration. Others would argue that his statement was born out of religious blindness and an ignorance of the Word of God. I believe that this pastor was sincere in his heart, but sincerely wrong. Why do I believe his thinking was in error? Does the prophetic comply with biblical standards for sound doctrine? Are the *Spirit of Christ* and the *gift of prophecy* synonymous?

Let us begin by outlining the existence of prophecy in the Bible. The words *prophet* and *prophets* are used nearly 600 times in the King James Version of the Bible. The words *prophecy*, *prophesy*, and *prophesied* are referred to over 160 times in Old and New Testament passages of scripture. In addition, there are many indirect references made in scripture pertaining to the prophetic.

In light of these numerous references, we must not ignore the existence of the prophetic in the Old and New Testaments. **From Genesis to Revelation, every book of the Bible is laden with prophetic implications.** Beginning with its first page, God Himself set the precedent when he prophetically declared, "Let there be light." The last page of the Bible ends with an admonishment from Jesus to heed "the words of prophecy of this book." Everything in between these two pages testifies to the fact that **the prophetic is embedded deep within the fabric of Scripture.**

Emergence of Old Testament Prophets

In the Old Testament prior to the prophets, all that Israel possessed in the form of God's will was the Law. The Lord had appeared to Moses on Mt. Sinai where He gave the Ten Commandments as a guide for moral and ethical behavior. In addition to the tablets of stone containing those commandments, Moses later compiled a list of ordinances, rites, duties, rules, and regulations. He gave further guidance by writing the first five books of the Bible, known as the *Torah*. Once in possession of these guidelines the people of God were expected to conduct their lives in a reasonable manner.

However, these laws did not specifically address many of the issues and situations which Israel would face. This was not due to any inherent weakness within the Law. Rather, it was due to the simple fact that it was impractical to address in detail every possible situation that would arise. **Hence, the establishment of prophets in the Old Testament emerged out of a great need to interpret the will of God for the nation of Israel.** God met this need by granting revelation to these prophets. Their function was to bring specific revelation to issues not covered by the Law. God used their prophetic gifts to expose hidden sins, to find the direction of God for Israel, to defeat their enemies in battle, and to give prophetic words to their generation.

Since these prophets spoke into current situations, it is often said that they functioned as forth-tellers (speaking forth a current message), not foretellers (speaking of things to come). However, it must not be forgotten that these prophets also spoke of the future. In many cases they predicted both future blessings and calamities for the nation of Israel.

For example, Isaiah spoke in beautiful language concerning the coming of the One who would save His people from their sins. Daniel, another Old Testament prophet, predicted the death of kings and the fall of kingdoms to come. He also prophesied the approximate time the Messiah would come. Consequently, both of these men were not only spokesmen for their generation (forth-tellers), but also prophetic seers who caught a glimpse of things which were yet to come.

Classification of Prophets

According to the *Pictorial Bible Dictionary*, pages 686-687, the books in the Hebrew Old Testament can be divided into three parts: the Law, the Prophets, and the Writings. The category known as the prophets can be further sub-divided into *former* and *latter prophets*.

Under the heading of *former* prophets we find Joshua, I and II Samuel, and I and II Kings. The authors of these books are anonymous, but history indicates that they were men who held prophetic office in ancient Israel. Inspired by the Holy Spirit, they wrote a detailed history of the period prior to the *latter* prophets. Without this history, it would be impossible to understand the works of such men as Isaiah and other great spokesmen.

Like the former prophets, the latter prophets were also known as writing prophets. The term *latter* does not necessarily refer to chronological history, but is a label given to prophetic books that follow the former prophets in the Hebrew Old Testament. Included in this category are Isaiah, Jeremiah and Ezekiel. These men were given some of the greatest ministries in the Old Testament.

However, these *latter* or *writing* prophets were not anonymous like the *former* prophets. They were called by God to deliver prophetic messages, not only to their generation, but for generations yet to come. Their names were made known to establish their credibility to future generations. Scripture does not speak of how these men prepared their messages. However, it seems as though they were, first of all, public speakers and secondly, writers (Jeremiah 30:1-2 seems to demonstrate that this order is likely). It could be that in many instances these prophets enlarged upon their oral messages by writing them down.

Whether anonymous or known, it must be understood that the former and latter prophets complemented one another. The former prophets set forth the history of a particular period in Israel's existence, while the latter prophets fulfilled parts of this history. In any case, their books stand as a testimony to the evidence of prophetic activity in the Old Testament.

School of the Prophets

When the people of Israel entered the Promised Land, "there was no king in Israel, everyone did what was right in his own eyes" (Judges 21:25).

In comparing themselves to other nations, Israel rejected God as its ruler and decided that they must have a king. "The elders of Israel...came to Samuel and said...'make us a king...like all the nations'...And, the Lord said to Samuel... 'they have not rejected you, but they have rejected me that I should not reign over them'" (I Sam. 8:4-7).

In compliance with Israel's demand, God gave them a king. Yet, the first king, Saul, was not a man after God's own heart, but was concerned with his own welfare. At the time of Saul's reign, Israel was endangered by the idolatry of Canaan and the militaristic advances of the Philistines. Hence, for the spiritual welfare of the nation, God raised up several companies, or schools of the prophets. It is assumed that this band of prophets spoke the Word of God to both king and commoner (I Sam. 19:19-20, II Kings 2:3-5).

It is difficult to say what is intended by the phrase "company of the prophets." Whether the groups of prophets had a formal organization is hard to tell. It may be that these groups were initially knit together serving under the supervision of the prophet Samuel. Although it cannot be positively stated that Samuel was the founder of these groups, such an assumption would seem to have much in its favor.

Following Samuel's death, these prophetic bands seemed to disappear until the times of Elijah and Elisha, where they suddenly appear again, bearing the title *sons of the prophets*. Apparently, this phrase revealed the close association between these groups of prophets and their relationship to Elijah and Elisha. After this, we hear no more of them (I Kings 20:35).

Description of Various Old Testament Prophets

There are various types of prophets found in the Old Testament. In theological terms, some of these men were given the title *major* prophets, while others were designated as *minor* prophets. Some were well-known for their ministry, while others seemed to be obscure. One thing is certain, **Like the colors in a rainbow, Old Testament prophets were as diverse in temperament as they were in calling.** Living in different environments and in different epochs of history, they were unique in every expression of their lives and ministries.

Their historical background varied from poor to rich, ignorant to educated, weak to strong, commoner to aristocrat. Yet, in spite of their diversity, there was a common thread woven throughout the tapestry of these prophets' lives. They were called by God and possessed a willingness to fulfill that calling. Like Moses, they were anointed by God to serve as His spokesmen to their generation.

Listed below is a brief biographical sketch of these prophets which I have attempted to compile in chronological order. Over the years, I have spent countless hours reflecting upon their nature, their character and the call of God upon the lives of these men. As a result, this has provided me with the breadth and depth I have needed to gain insight and understanding as to what God's call is upon my own life. Therefore, I strongly encourage those interested in the prophetic to develop an in-depth understanding of the life and times of our prophetic forefathers.

1.   ELIJAH - A miracle-working prophet who was fed by birds and angels, he raised the dead and called fire down from heaven.

2.   ELISHA - Had a double portion of Elijah's spirit. He performed miracles of healing and summoned angels. A dead man thrown on his grave was resurrected.

3.   JONAH - As a result of his prophetic ministry, the entire population of Nineveh repented, averting God's judgment for decades.

4.   AMOS - A colorful prophet who worked as a herdsman and rebuked Israel for idolatry.

5.   HOSEA - A highly educated prophet with great spiritual vision, both allegorical and direct.   God told him to marry a prostitute named Gomer as a sign.

6.   JOEL - He prophesied the future outpouring of God's Spirit upon all flesh, cited by Peter in Acts.

7.   ISAIAH - One of the most prolific prophets, he foretold the coming of the Messiah.   He is referred to as the *evangelist* of the Old Testament.

8.   MICAH - He prophetically spoke judgment as well as Messianic prophecy to Israel.

9.   OBADIAH - He is commonly described as a *minor* prophet who predicted the destruction of Edom.

10. NAHUM - He is acknowledged as a poetic prophet whose book some call a literary masterpiece.   He also predicted the destruction of Nineveh.

11. JEREMIAH - A compassionate prophet who is known as the "weeping prophet."   His writings were known as a book of prophetic sermons.

12. HABAKKUK - Possibly a Levitical musician, he prophesied utilizing a lyrical form.

13. ZEPHANIAH - A prophet of royal descent who held a prominent position within the nation.

14. DANIEL - Endowed with great wisdom, understanding and discernment, he received and interpreted dreams and had apocalyptic visions.

15. EZEKIEL - A powerful preacher who was both priest and prophet, he received many unusual visions and was commanded to dispense the prophetic in an equally unusual way.

16. ZECHARIAH - He was a priest and prophet who prophesied the destruction and restoration of Jerusalem. His writings consisted of eight symbolic visions.

17. HAGGAI - He prophesied the rebuilding of the House of God and declared that its latter glory would greatly exceed its former glory.

18. MALACHI - He was sent to correct the Levites, restore the Law and to declare that Elijah would come before the great and terrible day of the Lord.

New Testament Prophets

In the same way that prophets and prophecy thrived in the Old Testament era, they also flourished throughout the New Testament. For instance, Zacharias prophesied that his son, John the Baptist, would be called a prophet, preparing the way of the Messiah. Years later, John the Baptist would be recognized by his contemporaries as a major prophet. Jesus verified this claim by stating that John was the greatest prophet that ever lived. Our Lord also declared Himself to be a prophet fulfilling Moses' declaration that the Messiah would come in the office of a prophet to deliver Israel.(Luke 1:76, 7:26, 7:28, 13:33).

However, Joel had foretold a time when the gift of prophecy would be given to all believers. We see this word fulfilled at Pentecost. The Spirit descended and now all of God's people had the opportunity to be prophetic, for the gift was given to sons and daughters of Israel (Joel 2:28-29, Acts 2:17).

As a result of this prophetic outpouring, many things occurred. For instance, as the New Testament church matured, a diversity of gifts quickly emerged. There was a special power of utterance bestowed on some individuals (I Cor. 12:10), while others gravitated toward a ministry equal to the status of a prophet. It would be correct to say that all who spoke *the word of the Lord* were prophetic. Nevertheless, some were further distinguished in order that they might bear the prophet's mantle.

One such man was the apostle Paul. He was declared a prophet, in addition to being an apostle and teacher. The distinction between his prophetic ministry and the other two offices he held were as follows: while the apostle is a *sent one* who establishes and builds the Church, *the prophet is a messenger to the Church*. Whereas the teacher explains and enforces biblical truth, *the prophet is recognized by his hearers as a divine channel of fresh revelation*. (Note: This revelation is not extra-biblical revelation, but fresh light brought upon biblical truth.)

In addition to Paul, several New Testament prophets are specifically identified in Scripture. Judas and Silas were prophets at Antioch. Agabus and other prophets resided in Jerusalem. Philip the evangelist had four daughters who were highly prophetic. Others were also found moving about from church to church speaking the word of the Lord (Acts 11:27,28, 15:32, 21:9).

Finally, there was one who was endowed with literary prowess and committed his visions and revelations to writing. He is known as John the Revelator. Like Ezekiel in the Old Testament, this prophet/apostle recorded the revelation he received on the Isle of Patmos into what has become our Book of Revelation. This prophetic masterpiece is so profound that men of all religious persuasions acknowledge John the Revelator as a true prophet.

Jesus the Prophet

Revelation 19:10 states that, *"...The testimony of Jesus is the Spirit of prophecy."* <u>**Therefore, to acknowledge Jesus in scripture is to acknowledge prophecy.**</u> As already suggested, He is the embodiment of the prophetic. Thousands of years before His birth, Moses spoke of His prophetic nature, saying, "The Lord thy *God will raise up* unto thee *a prophet* from the midst of thee, of thy brethren, like unto me; unto him ye shall hearken" (Deut. 18:15, emphasis mine).

A close look at the life and ministry of Jesus will verify this prophecy spoken by Moses. Indeed, Jesus was considered a prophet by His contemporaries. He fulfilled prophecy, prophesied coming events, and flowed in the ministry of personal prophecy. In fact, every word Jesus spoke was pregnant with prophetic implications.

In the four gospels, there are dozens of references to Jesus' personal prophetic ministry. For instance, in John 1:48, He had revelatory knowledge concerning the whereabouts of Nathanael. In other passages of scripture, He had prophetic insight into the hidden motives of Peter's heart and perceived the colorful past of a Samaritan woman. Prior to resurrecting his friend Lazarus, He prophesied to the disciples and then again to Mary and Martha that Lazarus would rise from the dead as a testimony to God's power over death (Matt. 26:31-35, John 4:16-19, John 11:1-16).

Jesus also knew the thoughts of the Pharisees and foresaw the treachery of Judas. He foretold the destruction of Jerusalem and predicted the exact details of His own death and resurrection. Finally, as the Book of Revelation demonstrates, since His ascension, Jesus has continued to function in His role as Prophet to His Bride, the Church. And we are encouraged by His Spirit, through the Apostle Paul, to "Desire spiritual gifts, but rather that ye may *prophesy*" (Luke 11:17, John 13:27, Luke 21: 20-24, Matt. 12:40, John 12:32, I Cor. 14:1).

Summary

In response to the question asked in the beginning of this chapter (is the Bible our handbook for prophecy?), the answer is threefold. First, it is evident that Scripture validates prophetic ministry. Secondly, the Bible is a wonderful textbook from which we can learn the fundamentals of the prophetic. Finally, **when we establish our prophetic ministries in compliance with Scripture, we minimize the possibility of failing in the development of our skill.**

However, now that we understand the historical background and basic function of prophecy in the Bible, there are several questions which must be answered. What is the essence of prophecy today? How do we receive the gift of prophecy? Does it come to us through grace or works? And, how do we administrate the gift of prophecy? In the next chapter, I will attempt to answer these questions.

Chapter Three

THE GIFT OF PROPHECY

"Now concerning spiritual gifts, brethren, I would not have you ignorant." (I Cor. 12:1).

The very nature of the word *gift* implies that something has been freely given, without cost or expense. This is true in both biblical and secular language. For example, the New Testament word *gift* is often derived from the Greek word *charisma*, meaning a gratuity or grant. *Webster's Dictionary* also defines *gift* as "that which is bestowed voluntarily and without compensation; a present or endowment."

The Bible states in Romans 8:32, that God will "freely give us all things." The same is true of the "nine gifts of the Spirit," found in I Corinthians 12:8-10. In this portion of Scripture, the Apostle Paul declares that the word of wisdom, word of knowledge, faith, healings, miracles, prophecy, discerning of spirits, tongues, and interpretation of tongues are given by the Holy Spirit as He (the Spirit) sees fit. The implications are clear. **We cannot buy the gifts of the Spirit, bargain for them, or earn them. They are truly endowments of God and are imparted to His children, free of charge.**

The truth of God's free gift was made real to me as a young man. In the early 1970s, I had two friends who possessed a strong desire to receive and administer the gift of prophecy (one of the nine gifts of the Spirit mentioned in I Cor.). Each had sensed that he would one day minister this endowment to the church, however, neither of them knew how to receive or appropriate the gift. Driven by a passion to receive this gifting, one of my friends, who was unemployed, began to give himself to seasons of prayer and fasting. Periodically, he would spend days and weeks on his face before the Lord -- crying out for impartation.

39

My other friend, on the other hand, trusted the desires of his heart to God and continued to work a job, raise a family and minister part-time. Due to a busy schedule, he had very little time to launch an all-out assault on the throne of God. Other than occasional fasting and periodic seasons of prayer, he just "faithed it," believing that God's gift comes as a result of His grace.

Many years have passed since those days, and an amazing thing has happened. In spite of the different methods employed by my two friends, they are both presently flowing in the gift which they desired. I am convinced that one friend received his gifting not because of a dedication to *"pray it in,"* but because of God's sovereign choice. Likewise, my other friend's inability to pursue the gift of prophecy through prayer and fasting did not disqualify him from freely receiving it. Thus, time has proven what theory could only suggest: that **the impartation of spiritual gifts is not dependent upon performance or pressure from men.**

Did both friends have the proper attitude about spiritual gifts? Was one right to just believe God for His impartation? I believe so, but to those who might interpret my relaxed approach to the pursuit of spiritual gifts as being a lack of passion for God, I want to conclude this thought with two points.

First, it's true that Scripture encourages us to seek after the Lord, press into His Kingdom, pray without ceasing, etc. No Christian is exempt from this kind of radical pursuit of intimacy with our glorious God. However, the fact that we do these things doesn't mean that we qualify to receive the gifts of the Spirit. Rather, the only requirement for receiving is to "desire spiritual gifts" (1 Cor. 14:1).

Second, **when we pursue God through prayer and fasting, it should be for the purpose of knowing Him, not getting something from Him.** It's true, the Lord desires to give us the spiritual tools needed for ministry. But, as indicated, the gifts and callings of God are free and without repentance. They cannot be purchased by human sweat or endeavor. Once we have received these gifts, however, they can be enhanced -- honed to their fullest potential -- through the pursuit of intimacy with God by prayer and meditation upon His word.

I Corinthians Gifts of The Spirit

There are three classifications of spiritual gifts found in I Corinthians 12:8-10. They are described by some as power gifts, revelation gifts, and utterance gifts.

1. Power gifts include:

    a. *Miracles:* the ability to perform supernatural signs and wonders.

    b. *Gifts of healing:* the ability to cure various ailments and diseases.

    c. *Faith:* the ability to act like God in "calling those things that are not as though they are."

2. Revelation gifts include:

    a. *Word of wisdom:* the ability to discern the proper wisdom for a person or situation.

    b. *Word of knowledge:* the ability to discern things known to others but at the time unknown to you.

    c. *Discerning of spirits:* the ability to discern the presence of spirits, both good and bad.

3. Utterance gifts include:

    a. *Tongues:* the ability to speak an unlearned tongue or dialect.

b. *Interpretation of tongues:* the ability to translate an unlearned tongue or dialect.

c. *Prophecy:* the ability to see and predict the future, also to declare the revealed word of God.

Although all nine of these gifts are vital to the Body of Christ, the gift of prophecy appears to be highlighted by Paul in his writings to the Corinthian Church. For instance, in I Corinthians 14:1 he instructs us, "Desire spiritual gifts, but rather that ye may prophesy." Two things are apparent in this Scripture. First, there is an understanding that the believer has access to all spiritual gifts. Otherwise, we would not be encouraged to desire something we couldn't have. Second, Paul, by the inspiration of the Spirit, singles out prophecy and gives it priority over the other gifts. He further stresses the importance of this gift by declaring in verse 5, "...Greater is he that prophesieth...."

In light of the importance given to prophecy in these two Scriptures, and in keeping with the prophetic theme of this book, I want to focus solely upon the gift of prophecy. However, any attempt to define prophecy is highly complicated by the two other revelation gifts which overlap and blend with the gift of prophecy. These gifts are the word of wisdom and the word of knowledge. In many instances, all three of these gifts flow together in a prophetic stream, making it difficult to distinguish one from the other.

In spite of their compatibility to the gift of prophecy, we will not define the word of knowledge and the word of wisdom in this chapter. Our priority is prophecy -- our goal is to understand its use.

Prophecy Defined

I have often been asked the question, *"What is prophecy and how do we flow in it?"* To answer this question we must begin with the basics. *Strong's Exhaustive Concordance of the Bible* defines the Greek words *propheteis* and *prophetcuo* -- prophecy and prophesy -- in this manner: "to predict, to foretell, to speak under inspiration."

According to *Scribner's Dictionary of the Bible,* the most frequently used word to describe prophecy in the Old Testament is *nabi.* This Hebrew word was used over 300 times and was long associated with a root which meant to *bubble up.* It is *now* more usually connected with a kindred Arabic word meaning *to announce.* References such as *Irwin's Bible Commentary* verify this by interpreting prophecy, "The declaring of God's will, whether for the present or the future." In *Scribner's Dictionary of the Bible,* prophecy is described as, "Authoritative announcement of the Divine will in a particular case."

I'm sure there are many other valid references as to the meaning of prophecy. Yet all of these can be reduced to one simple thought: **Prophecy is God speaking through man**. This truth is substantiated in 430 instances throughout the Old Testament where prophetic figures declared, "Thus saith the Lord." Peter exemplifies this dynamic in the New Testament by writing, "If a man speak, let him speak as the oracles of God" (I Peter 4:11).

However, before we become God's mouthpiece, there are two characteristics unique to the gift of prophecy, which we must understand. First, there is a requirement which we must fulfill prior to flowing in this gift found in I Cor. 12:10. This requirement is the infilling of the Spirit, known also as the baptism of the Holy Spirit. Second, unlike the Old Testament examples in which the Spirit fell upon men and they then began prophesying, it appears that once New Testament believers have received the infilling of the Spirit, the gift of prophecy lies resident within. As a result of this abiding anointing, we have the capacity to prophesy when and where the Spirit desires.

Now that we have identified the two principles associated with the gift of prophecy, let us examine the first: namely, that the

…spirit precedes the gifts of the Spirit. This is clearly 19:1-6 where Paul asked the Christians at Ephesus, "D… …ceive the Holy Spirit when you believed?' And they said, …, we have never even heard that there is a Holy Spirit' …and when Paul had laid his hands upon them, the Holy Spirit came upon them; and they spoke with tongues and prophesied."

In addition to Acts 19, several other New Testament Scriptures tend to promote the concept of baptism before gift. In Luke 1:67, Zacharias, the father of John the Baptist, was filled with the Holy Spirit and prophesied. In Acts 2:1-36, Peter descends from the Upper Room on the day of Pentecost and, being freshly baptized in the Holy Spirit, prophesies from the book of Joel. Please note that they flowed in prophecy only after receiving the Holy Spirit as a second experience to salvation. The formula was: Salvation + Baptism of the Spirit = an open channel for prophecy to flow.

The Resident Gift

Let us now look at the second principle, which we will call the *resident anointing.* For those who have received the infilling of the Spirit, this dynamic enables them to draw, at all times, upon the gift which dwells within their spirit.

Unlike Old Testament prophecy that came as a result of outward stimulation, the New Testament gift operates as a result of an inward witness and inner prompting of the Holy Spirit. The one is an anointing which comes *upon us* (Old Testament). The other is an anointing which dwells *within us* (New Testament). This contrast between the Old Testament and the New Testament anointing is outlined by the scriptural references below.

OLD TESTAMENT: Num. 11:25: The spirit rested *upon* them
NEW TESTAMENT: Col. 1:27: Christ *in* you the hope of glory

OLD TESTAMENT: Isa. 42:1: I have put My Spirit *upon* him
NEW TESTAMENT: Eph. 3:17: Christ may dwell *in* your hearts

OLD TESTAMENT: EZE. 6:1: Word of the Lord came **unto** me
NEW TESTAMENT: COL. 3:16: Word of Christ dwell **in** you

OLD TESTAMENT: EZE. 11:5: Spirit of the Lord fell **upon** me
NEW TESTAMENT: ACTS 2:4: They were **filled** with the Spirit

OLD TESTAMENT: Isa. 61:1: The Spirit of the Lord is **upon** me
NEW TESTAMENT: I JN. 2:27: The anointing...abideth **in** you

OLD TESTAMENT: II KINGS 2:15: Spirit of Elijah doth rest **on**
NEW TESTAMENT: JOHN 14:17: Spirit of Truth...shall be **in** you

In light of these Scriptures, it could be said that <u>the same anointing which rested upon the prophets of old, is now resident within the believer</u>. Unlike our spiritual forefathers we, as Spirit-filled Christians, are no longer limited to relying upon an external manifestation of God's Spirit. Instead, we can look to the well of living water that resides within us, and, at any time, apply it to the need. Whether it be healing, faith, prophecy, etc., the manifestation will come from the Christ who lives **in us**, not the Christ who is seated **above us**.

Over the years, I have relied heavily upon this principle of the *abiding anointing*. Nevertheless, I came by this lesson the hard way. Before learning to appropriate the *gift within*, I spent a lot of time in prayer and fasting. My expectation was for the Spirit of God to fall upon me and direct me. I can remember kneeling on my knees awaiting a sign from heaven -- something like a vision, an angel or an audible voice from God. I was determined to receive my word from God in the natural realm of sight, touch, or sound.

In spite of my persistence, nothing tangible ever seemed to manifest. Weary and frustrated, I would finally get up and go about my everyday business. Then, much to my surprise, the word I so desperately needed would begin to arise out of the depths of my spirit. It seemed that I had an inner witness, confirming what I should do and where I should go. I soon learned that my answers seldom came by way of outer manifestation of the supernatural. Instead, they came out of the *ever abiding word of the Lord* that lived within me. As a result, I began to trust this inner witness as opposed to relying upon an outer manifestation.

(Note: The fact that God didn't choose to reveal Himself to me in a visible or audible way, didn't cause me to abandon my pursuit of God through prayer and fasting. In fact, I strongly believe that prayer and fasting dials down the clamor of our soul and heightens our ability to hear and be led by the inner witness of the Holy Spirit.)

A Step Beyond

It's one thing to recognize the abiding gift of prophecy and yet another to use it accurately and precisely. As believers, we must be sensitive to this issue and endeavor to represent, as best we can, the true heart of the Lord. **Before we express ourselves prophetically, there needs to be an awareness that we are speaking for a God who is complex in nature, advanced in communication, and shrouded with mystery.**

However, to exercise this kind of prophetic utterance, which is a step beyond the I Corinthians 12:10 gift of prophecy, a few things are necessary. As mentioned, we are faced with the difficulty of representing a God whom we hardly know or understand. Although this skill is not yet necessary for young believers who operate in a beginner's level of prophecy, it is absolutely essential for maturing prophets. Those who flow in deeper dimensions of prophetic expression should know that more is required of those "who have been given much" (Luke 12:48).

Over the years, I have spent countless hours meditating upon the inherent difficulty of this task. How can we articulate with any degree of accuracy the heart of a God whom we cannot see or

46

touch? If prophecy is the vehicle by which we express the thoughts of God, then how can we translate into human dialect that which we receive from God? **Any attempt to capture the heart of God in human language would be like trying to thread the universe through the eye of a needle.**

God is a spiritual entity, not a human being. As one writer put it, His ways are not our ways, neither are His thoughts our thoughts. He does not think like a human, act like a human, or live in the realm of human experience. His first language is not English, German, Spanish, African, French or any other kind of earthly tongue. It's true that He often converses with us on a human level but, in reality, He is capable of a communication form that is light-years beyond the realm of human thought or articulation. In a split second, He can convey by His Spirit, more information than we could enunciate in a thousand years. The apostle Paul testifies to this in II Corinthians 12:2-4:

> Fourteen years ago I was taken up to heaven for a visit, don't ask me whether my body was there or just my spirit, for I don't know. Only God can answer that. But anyway there I was in paradise, and heard things so astounding that they are beyond a man's power to describe or put in words (The Living Bible).

Reception vs. Perception

If we bear in mind the difficulty of expressing spiritual things with the human tongue, how then do we flow in our resident gift of prophecy? First, we must understand the difference between Old and New Testament prophecy. **Old Testament prophecy is revelation received, whereas New Testament prophecy is revelation perceived.** Both are inspired by God, but each exists within a different dispensation of time. One is before Christ, the other after Christ.

47

For example, Old Testament prophets declared hundreds of times "Thus saith the Lord," as if they were repeating -- word for word, statements received in their own language. On the other hand, there isn't one instance in the New Testament where believers said, "Thus saith the Lord." It's true that God spoke to many New Covenant prophets in the first century Church, but the absence of "Thus saith the Lord" seems to indicate a different kind of prophetic flow.

Expressions like, "and this I speak...and I think also that I have the Spirit of God," or "It seemed good to the Holy Spirit, and to us," or "The Spirit speaketh expressly," and "I say the truth in Christ...my conscience bearing me witness in the Holy Spirit" appeared to be the rule for prophetic expression in the New Testament Church (I Cor. 7:35, 40; Acts 15:28; I Tim. 4:1; and Rom. 9:1).

In light of these Scriptures, **the New Testament "gift of prophecy" carries with it the privilege of interpreting the thought and intent of God's heart.** It is not merely the act of repeating exact statements as dictated by God in the Old Testament (*revelation received*). Rather, it is the ability to perceive God's heart and articulate it (*revelation perceived*). Initially the thought will come from the heart of God, but through the process of translation it will be filtered through our intellect, language, personality, etc.

Finally, the most significant difference between *revelation received* and *revelation perceived* is that **we, as believers under the New Covenant, have a greater latitude of expression than did our Old Testament counterparts.** Even so, this freedom comes as a result of an intimate relationship with the Lord. Therefore, if we fail to develop that intimacy, we run the risk of misinterpreting or misrepresenting His heart.

Applying the Principle

Those who are intimate with Jesus must believe that their thoughts, hearts, and native tongues can be inspired by the Spirit of God. As a result, they are capable of imparting the prophetic in a manner which is independent of their own self righteousness. Why? Because **God has chosen to express Himself through the frailty of mankind despite our inadequacies and sinful tendencies:**

> For it was not through any human whim that
> man prophesied of old; men they were, but,
> impelled by the Holy Spirit, they spoke the words
> of God (II Peter 1:21, New English Bible).

In light of this Scripture, I have learned to conduct my prophetic ministry in today's church in much the same way. I know that I am just a man, and I am aware of the difficulties of expressing God's fullness with the human tongue. I know in part, I prophesy in part, but in spite of all these limitations I am able to flow in a legitimate form of the prophetic.

However, I usually precede any attempt to relate a prophetic word to people by using words like "I perceive," "I sense" and "I discern." Seldom do I say, "Thus saith the Lord," or repeat a preprogrammed word. Why? **We are not prophetic puppets on a string. Rather, we are the children of God, learning to interpret the heart of our Father and express it the best we can. We are uniquely different from other prophetic figures and original in our delivery.** When prophesying, it may be our mouth, our voice, and our words, yet the inspiration comes from God and is birthed out of intimacy with Him.

Does this mean that we are free to prophetically express ourselves as we choose? Absolutely not! It would be a great mistake to presume that God will validate every word that we speak. Neither will He bless believers who prophesy anything that

49

pops into their head. It's true, some of these Christians may accidentally stumble onto the word of the Lord or occasionally lock into a stream of prophecy, but, bear in mind, **prophetic maturity is a skill which is developed by those who spend time with God.**

Summary

In this chapter we have determined that prophecy is an endowment to the church -- a free gift from God. We also learned that prophecy is God speaking through man and that the New Testament gift of prophecy is resident within the believer. Furthermore, we determined that the exercise of this gift under the New Covenant, gives us the privilege of interpreting the thought and intent of God's heart.

However, it's one thing to understand the definition and use of prophecy and yet another to understand the significance of its role in the church. Therefore, a question of priority arises. Does prophecy have a greater value than the other nine gifts of the Spirit?

We briefly mentioned in this chapter, that the Apostle Paul described prophecy as the greater gift. How could Paul say such a thing? It seems to me that, in a general sense, the greatest gift is the one needed at the moment. For example, a person dying of a dreaded disease would most likely benefit more from someone with a gift of healing rather than someone accurately prophesying the details of their lives. Nevertheless, the Apostle Paul clearly states in I Cor. 14:5 that, in comparison to the gift of tongues, prophecy is greater in usefulness. Therefore, in the following chapter we shall examine what Paul meant.

Chapter Four

PROPHECY: THE GREATER GIFT

> I wish you all had the gift of speaking in tongues but, even more, I wish you were able to prophesy, preaching God's messages, for that is a greater and more useful power than to speak in unknown languages... (I Cor. 14:5, The Living Bible).

As a young child, I spent hundreds of hours sitting in the pews of our little church. There were times when I was just plain bored, and other times when I was captivated by the moving of the Holy Spirit. During those times of spiritual outpouring, I would be perched on my seat, like a bird on a wire. With intense curiosity, I would observe the manifestation of spiritual gifts as they surfaced within the meetings.

On those occasions when God chose to manifest Himself, people would be saved, healed, delivered, and baptized in the Spirit. During these times, certain members of the church would become overly excited about what was happening and burst forth in a strange language known as the gift of tongues. Then, everything would stop as people bowed their heads in awe of an utterance from God.

At the time, I was unable to understand the importance that our congregation attached to these strange tongues. However, I learned to accept them. What choice did I have? I was told that the public expression of tongues during the service was God speaking to the church. If that were true, I thought, then who was I to contend with the Almighty? If He wished to speak in gibberish, then I supposed I should listen. However, I could never figure out why God would talk to me in a language which I could neither recognize nor understand. Even for a child, this seemed a little strange.

51

Tongues In Context

There is an amazing quality which resides within the heart of most children. It seems as though they have a sixth sense which enables them to navigate through the treacherous waters of fallacious thinking. Adults may be fooled indefinitely, but children seem to know when things are not quite right. They may not fully understand what they are sensing nor can they articulate it, but later in life they find out that the uneasy feeling within their heart was nothing less than discernment in its purest form.

The same was true of my experience with the use of tongues in our little church. I had no theology to support my gut feeling, but I knew there was more to God's voice than a vague utterance in unknown tongues. I suspected that a God who could speak in any language would not limit Himself to only one form of communication.

Don't get me wrong! I believe in speaking in tongues and appreciate its place in the Christian experience. However, I am convinced, like the apostle Paul, that tongues must be used in a way that is beneficial for the Church.

> "Even in the case of inanimate objects which are capable of making sound, such as a flute or harp, unless their notes have the proper intervals, who can tell what tune is being played on them?...So, in your case, unless you make intelligible sounds with your tongue how can anyone know what you are talking about? You may as well be addressing an empty room" (I Corinthians 14:7-9, Phillips Modern English).

What is Paul saying? Is he suggesting there is no value in speaking in tongues? No, in fact he validates tongues by charging the church to *"Forbid not to speak in tongues."* Speaking out of personal experience he also said, "I thank my God, I speak with tongues more than ye all." So, Paul's contention was not with

52

tongues, per se, but with the misuse of them in public meetings, especially when there is no interpretation for the tongue spoken. That is why he pleaded with those who spoke in tongues to "pray that he may interpret" (I Cor. 14: 39, 14:18, 14:13).

Setting Order

According to I Cor. 14, there was obviously a misuse of tongues within the Corinthian Church. The outpouring of the Spirit had impacted the believers in such a way that most were overcome with a feverish desire to exercise their gifts publicly. As a result, the Corinthians began to speak in tongues simultaneously, leaving very little room for an interpretation. Knowing the confusion that was created by these ecstatic utterances, Paul was faced with the task of "setting divine order."

Paul's concern was twofold. First, how could he encourage the operation of this gift and at the same time prevent the mass confusion that arose as a result of overzealous tongue-talkers? Second, was it possible to convince the unbelievers as to the validity of "spiritual gifts?"

Paul demonstrated his wisdom and apostolic authority when he proclaimed a seemingly simple solution to this complex problem in Corinth. Concerning the first issue he wrote: "

If the question of speaking with a tongue arises, confine the speaking to two or three at the most. They must speak in turn and have someone to interpret what is said. If you have no interpreter then let the speaker with a tongue keep silent in the church and speak only to himself and God (I Cor. 14:27-28, Phillips Modern English).

Paul clarifies the remaining issue in this manner:

So if the whole congregation is assembled and all are using the strange tongues of ecstasy, and some uninstructed persons or unbelievers should enter, will they not think you are mad? But if all are uttering prophecies, the visitor, when he enters, hears from everyone something that searches his conscience and brings conviction, and the secrets of his heart are laid bare. So he will fall down and worship God, crying "God is certainly among you" (I Cor. 14:23-25, New English Bible).

Inspiration vs. Information

Just because a word is _inspirational_, doesn't mean that it's _informational._ The same is true of an utterance in tongues that is not accompanied with an interpretation. In many instances, this expression in tongues can inspire our spirit and soul but all too often our minds are left in the dark. Therefore, to minister to the whole man, both of these dynamics are essential. There must be information for the mind and inspiration for the spirit -- one cannot do without the other.

For example, if one has inspiration only, the mind, being unfruitful falls into a passive state of idleness. On the other hand, if there is too much information, the mind can be active and enlightened while one's spirit starves from a lack of inspiration. For this reason, there must be a marriage between inspiration and information.

Recently, I was faced with this dilemma while attending a conference in Southern California. A friend of mine who was conducting the meetings had arranged for my wife and I to attend some of the nightly sessions. On the first night, when it was time for personal ministry, I was summoned onto the platform by my friend and other ministers who were present. I was then told that I would receive encouragement from the Lord.

Since I was desperate for a word from God, I quickly grabbed my wife's hand, moved into position and expected the best. With my head bowed and my hands lifted high in the air, I assumed the well-known charismatic aren't-I-humble? posture. I was now ready to receive a prophetic word which had the potential to knock my socks off.

At this time a wild-eyed husband and wife team began to circle my wife and I like a Hollywood portrayal of Indians circling a wagon train. After much hoopla, they descended upon us, ready to deliver the word of the Lord. What happened next was no less than a "prophetic scalping." One of them laid their hands on my head while the other began a war hoop in unknown tongues. The longer they prayed, the louder they became.

Finally, after ten minutes of rapid-fire tongues, they seemed to run out of ammunition. As a strange quietness filled the room, I took a deep breath and braced myself for the interpretation. But much to my surprise the couple huddled together, conducted a spiritual powwow, and then left the stage. Their attitude seemed to indicate that it was God who had spoken and they were under no obligation to give an interpretation.

I'll never forget the feelings I had that night. I was irritated, frustrated, disillusioned, and totally embarrassed. Most of all, I was disappointed in having received a "word from God" that made absolutely no sense. Although it was quite an emotional experience it failed to bring understanding to my natural mind.

Since then, I have often thought of how the Apostle Paul would have reacted in that situation. I have come to the conclusion that this couple would not have escaped without a strong exhortation concerning the proper use of spiritual gifts. As a result, the next time they attempted to speak for God it would be done in a way that would benefit those receiving the word.

Tongues vs. Prophecy

...For greater is he that prophesieth, than he that speaketh with tongues... (I Cor. 14:5).

55

There are two distinct thoughts which emerge simultaneously from 1 Corinthians, chapter 14. We have already identified one as being the excessive use of tongues without an interpretation. The second thought, which is embodied in verse 5 of this chapter, is sometimes more difficult for believers to accept. This thought implies that prophecy has priority over tongues.

Upon close examination of I Corinthians 14:5, it is evident that, in a church setting, the use of the prophetic gift is superior to the gift of tongues. The key word used to support this concept is the Greek word *meizon*, which is translated in most English Bibles as *greater*. In a broad sense it also means *larger*, or could have been translated *elder*. In any case, the expanded thought could be expressed as follows: *He who prophesies is greater or more mature than he who speaks with tongues.*

The reasoning behind Paul's argument in 1 Cor. 14:5 is quite obvious. It wasn't a matter of personal preference that motivated him to exalt prophecy over tongues, but rather a desire to see the whole church blessed with a clear word from God. If this could have been done through unknown utterances, then I'm sure he would have had no problem declaring tongues as the greater gift.

However, as we all know, Paul declares elsewhere in Scripture, "He that speaketh in an *unknown tongue* speaketh not unto men, but unto God. For no man understandeth him...but he that prophesieth speaketh unto men to edification, and exhortation, and comfort." Paul concludes his thought in I Cor. 14:4 by writing, "He that speaketh in an *unknown tongue* edifies himself; but he that prophesieth edifies the Church." Consequently, the real issue is the use of tongues for self-edification versus edification of the whole church through prophecy. In this context, prophecy becomes the greater gift.

(Note: There is a definite distinction made between the unknown tongue and the gift of tongues. While the unknown

56

tongue is a personal prayer language spoken in unintelligible form and having no apparent interpretation, the gift of tongues is the ability to utter known languages with the expectation that there will be an interpretation. This is why Paul discourages the use of unknown tongues with no interpretation in a public setting and encourages the gift of tongues, accompanied with an interpretation, in a church meeting.)

Making The Transition

Scripture teaches that it is always more blessed to give than to receive. I theorize that these words were in the back of Paul's mind when he instructed the Corinthians on tongues and prophecy. The proof is seen in the way he attempted to divide them into two categories: the tongue - talkers who were content to encourage themselves and those who unselfishly prophesy as a blessing to others. In any case it's clear that most Spirit-filled Christians, both then and now, fall into one of these categories or the other.

I first experienced this principle of tongues vs. prophecy many years ago as a young preacher. It all began in the early 1970's when I first launched my ministry as a staff pastor in a charismatic church. I couldn't preach or pastor very well, but I had two other things going for me. I was accomplished in tongue-talking and possessed the knock-em-down anointing.

For those who may not understand the terminology knock-em-down, the phrase was used to describe a 1970's phenomenon in which people were slain in the Spirit (rendered unconscious) by the laying on of hands. I'm not sure of the connection between speaking in tongues and being slain in the Spirit, but the one seemed to enhance the other. Whatever the association, God often used me to accomplish both.

However, I rarely pastored my church in the traditional sense. I hardly ever visited newcomers, counseled with the sheep, kissed their babies, married the young couples, or buried the dead. I just gave myself to the ecstasy of praying in unknown utterances. Of course, I deeply loved the flock, but their mid-week crises seemed to distract me from what I considered to be my first calling — praying in tongues.

My reasoning was simple. Without an over-indulgence in tongues (which I desperately needed to strengthen myself), I would never have made it as a believer, much less as a minister. My concern was not to fix every little problem in the church, but to build myself up in the most holy faith by praying in tongues. *And why should this not be a priority?* I thought. *Come Sunday morning there were people to knock down. So if I didn't pray in tongues, many of them would be left standing as a testimony to my lack of anointing.* With this mentality, I often forced myself into countless hours of private tongue-talking.

Oftentimes, after reaching a high plateau of spiritual ecstasy in prayer, I would arise like an Old West gunslinger ready to do battle. I would saddle my old pinto car and, with Bible in hand, ride into the sunset looming over our Sunday night service. When I arrived at the church, I didn't even say hello to the boys that were hanging around the corral. I just dismounted from my car and, like a spiritual John Wayne, burst through the church doors with both guns drawn.

Occasionally, without even preaching, I would begin to line the church up in a row as though they were ducks in a shooting gallery. Big, small, young or old -- it didn't matter to me, none could escape the anointing that blazed out of my spiritual trigger finger. One by one I would move down the line of people, speaking in tongues and knocking them down on the floor. Finally, when I had emptied all my spiritual guns, I would holster my smoking fingers and ride out of town without saying another word. If anybody wanted to find me, I would be hiding in my prayer closet, reloading for the next big shoot-out.

58

It was during one of these prayer times that the Lord began to speak to me about my methods of ministry. One night while praying in tongues, I was interrupted by a voice that said, "Son what are you doing?" Although I knew this was the Lord speaking to me, I was unsettled by the nature of the question. I remember thinking, *If God doesn't know what I am doing then I must really be in trouble!* I replied, "Lord I'm doing what your word says — speaking in tongues."

At this point He asked me a second question that was even more unsettling than the first. He said, "Son, do you know what you are praying about?" Again my answer was scriptural as I replied, "Lord, my understanding is unfruitful, but my spirit knows exactly what I'm saying." That was the last time I got a chance to respond in the conversation!

In a loving way, God began to explain to me the finer points of mature ministry. He indicated that I had been using His anointing primarily to put people to sleep whereas His desire was to awaken them to the truth. He said, *"Knocking people unconscious on the floor is fine, but the greater need is to resurrect the saints so they might hear what the Spirit is saying to the church."* He continued to instruct me in this matter, urging me to use my native tongue when ministering to the church. I would be allowed to continue knocking them down, He implied, but I must also give them an intelligible word from the Lord.

I wasn't able to fully understand the implications of my little talk with God at that time. But I did begin to make a transition from tongues to prophecy. In fact, the very next Sunday when people came forward to be slain in the Spirit, I refrained from speaking to them in tongues. It was hard to break my previous habit, but, nevertheless, I flowed in the greater gift by uttering simple words of prophecy to two or three people.

I'm not convinced that my words greatly impacted anyone that day. However, I am convinced that I made the proper adjustment in

59

the administration of my ministry. From that day forward, I gained greater understanding of the significant role that prophecy plays within the church. This experience created a desire within me to encourage others to exercise the gift of prophecy as well as the gift of tongues.

However, my zeal to lead people into the prophetic was soon stifled by questions relating to who can prophesy. I was often asked, "Is prophetic expression exclusively relegated to mature believers among the male leadership? Can women and children prophesy? And, if so, how do we nurture and raise up the prophetic within the greater Body of Christ?" These are the issues we shall explore in the next chapter.

Chapter Five

WHO CAN PROPHESY?

In today's Church, people are asking serious questions about the ownership of prophecy. Is the whole Church called to the prophetic? If so, then who can prophesy? Do sheep have the same privileges as shepherds? What is the role of women in prophetic ministry? Can children speak prophetically? These are some of the issues that transcend cultural and ecclesiastical barriers and stir up controversy within the entire Body of Christ.

In the last few years, I have witnessed more quarrels, hurt feelings, and church splits over the issue of who can prophesy than any other issue encompassing the prophetic. This conflict has defiled the hearts of many of our best pastors. And, in turn, some of the most loyal sheep have developed attitude problems that border upon sheer rebellion. Forbidden to prophesy, they have strayed from their sheepfolds (churches) in search of greener prophetic pastures.

In most instances, whether male or female, the opinion of prophetic sheep is unanimous. They sincerely believe that most leaders are overly controlling and heavy-handed with prophetic people. For example, many prophetic females feel suppressed by what they believe to be egotistical, male-dominated clergy. We know this is not true of all ministers. However, the fears of these sheep seem to be heightened by the attitudes of a few pastors and elders who are opposed to any kind of prophetic flow within their churches. Especially damaging are those leaders who deny the right of exercising the gift of prophecy to anyone but themselves.

Why have a number of church leaders seemingly cornered the market on prophecy? Do they have any scriptural basis for their actions? Of course not! Paul states in I Cor. 14:1 that all may prophesy. Nevertheless, some of these leaders believe that it's their role to protect the Church from the weirdness that surrounds certain prophetic people. They are convinced that the gift of prophecy is dangerous in the hands of undeveloped sheep. As a result, only the designated *mature ones* (elders, deacons, associates, etc.) can prophesy. All others must sit in silence and hope for the day that their elders determine that they are mature enough to be released in their gifting.

This sort of unwritten theology seems to dominate the realm of ecclesiastical thinking. As indicated, the underlying logic may seem reasonable, but the outcome is counterproductive to prophetic growth in the Church. Therefore, the apostle Paul instructs us in I Cor. 14:31 to prophesy, "one by one, that all may learn." His emphasis wasn't on the theological perfection of prophecy, but on training those who are developing in the use of prophetic utterance.

However, to those who are committed to theological purity and have seen the abuse of those who advocate this view, I readily agree that there is a tremendous need to handle the prophetic with reverence and godly wisdom. By no means should we allow those who are immature to deliberately bring a reproach upon the name of the Lord. Nor should beginners bear the responsibility for giving prophetic words of correction or direction. **Yet, basic prophetic encouragement such as edification, exhortation, and comfort belong to all who have a heart to build up the Body of Christ.**

> But there remained two of the men in the camp, the name of the one was Eldad, and the name of the other Medad...and they prophesied in the camp. And there ran a young man, and told Moses, and said, "Eldad and Medad do prophesy in the camp." And Joshua the son of Nun, the servant of Moses, one of his young men, answered and said, "my Lord Moses, forbid them." And Moses said unto him, "Enviest thou for my sake? *Would to God that all the Lord's people were prophets, and that the Lord would put His Spirit upon them.*" (Num. 11:26-29, emphasis mine).

Maturity vs. Availability

The issue of who can flow in the prophetic does not always revolve around maturity or eldership, but around availability. In fact, it was often the common folk and new converts in the New Testament who prophesied under the inspiration of the Holy Spirit. They prophesied not because they were schooled, experienced, or mature in prophecy, but because they were available.

The Apostle Paul understood this principle and instructed the Corinthian church that "...all may prophesy..." (I Cor. 14:31). His exhortation to prophesy was not directed to a handful of mature leaders, but to all who were open and accessible. In the Book of Acts he demonstrated this truth by laying hands on common believers and imparting the Holy Spirit to them. As a result, they also prophesied.

There are other instances in the Bible where this concept is illustrated. For example, in the Old Testament, availability seemed to characterize the life and ministry of Moses. In the book of Exodus, this principle of availability is demonstrated when both Moses and his younger brother yield to a prophetic calling from God.

Initially, God appeared to Moses at a burning bush and appointed him as a prophet/deliverer to Israel. However, Moses felt incapable of fulfilling this great commission by himself and petitioned the Lord for a helper. As a result Aaron, his brother, came under the umbrella of Moses' calling and took command of the prophetic office. Aaron became God's spokesman, not because he was tremendously talented or even experienced, but because he was available. Therefore, Moses and Aaron labored together as one of the first prophetic teams.

In the book of Numbers, we see further indications that prophetic anointing was given to other men who were yielded to the Spirit of God. In addition to Aaron, seventy elders also received a prophetic mantle. It is recorded in Numbers 11:25 that, "the Lord came down in a cloud, and spoke unto him [Moses], and took of the Spirit that was upon him and gave it unto the seventy elders: And it came to pass, that, when the Spirit rested upon them, they prophesied and did not cease."

Again, in my opinion, these seventy elders received prophetic impartation not because they were special, but because they were open to receive from God. They were in the right place at the right time and display a willingness to accommodate their leader. Consequently, they not only prophesied, but operated under Moses' mantle of authority for the rest of their lives.

Like Aaron and the seventy elders, we too, must be available to the ministry of the Holy Spirit. We must not be as concerned with who can prophesy, as we are with when and where we can prophesy. We must understand that in God's kingdom both sheep and shepherd, the mature and immature, the educated and uneducated, are released to flow in prophetic utterance.

Male and Female

We shall now turn our attention to one of the more volatile issues of the Church today — the role of women in ministry. Does the Bible encourage women to prophesy? Do they have authority to address the church prophetically? Can they hold prophetic office? Before I answer these questions, I would like to note that much of my thinking presented in the next few pages was inspired by reading *The Apostle Paul And Women In The Church*, by Dr. Don Williams, published by Regal Books, 1977.

Some believe the writings of the apostle Paul prohibit women from participating in spiritual ministry, other than an occasional utterance of prophecy. Others are of the opinion that Paul had a heart to affirm women in ministry, but was hindered by the culture and traditions of his day. Before we discuss these issues, let us begin by reviewing the controversial role of women in the New

Testament. I must warn you that discussion of this topic can be passionate, since the issues of submission and biblical authority arise.

How can the Bible be the infallible Word of God if one assumes that its writers seemed to lean toward ancient custom? Where do we draw the line between eternal truth and cultural truth? Were the writers of the Bible merely responding to the needs of their generation? And, if men of God, like the apostle Paul, are wrong about women's roles, how can we trust the rest of their writings?

Questions on submission, authority, family, and church gatherings also surface. Does the Bible advocate merely a domestic role for women? What is a woman's role, if any, in the church? Is the ordination of women a direct violation of divine order? Needless to say, the answers given are usually conflicting and confusing. As a result, these issues have seriously divided believers and whole denominations.

However, the conflict over a *woman's place* is nothing new to the Church. As indicated, centuries ago the apostle Paul was caught in the eye of this storm. In wrestling with this issue, Paul seems to be lost in the theological whirlwind of affirming and disavowing women in ministry. On one hand, Paul positions himself as an advocate for women's roles as wife and mother. On the other hand, he crusades for the rights of women by liberating them from a demeaning Jewish culture. At times, Paul was adamant, demanding women to be veiled, silent and subordinate to men. Yet in Galatians 3:28, he sets women free by declaring, "There is neither male nor female in Christ."

Paul never allowed a woman to be ordained, but quite often he spoke affectionately of women who were co-laborers in the Gospel. As indicated, these contrasting positions have been painfully frustrating for women and men alike. As a result of this paradox, the attitude of today's church toward women in ministry swings from one end of the pendulum to the other. So extreme are the opinions of some, that a literal war of words has developed between the two sides. The one side strongly demands the equality of women in the church, while the other dogmatically denies the ministerial office to any female.

Consequently, these two positions have polarized many people within various denominations. For instance, the Catholic church has long denied women the right of ordination into priesthood. In contrast, the Episcopal church has a history of ordaining women into priesthood. With these kinds of extremes, it is no wonder that the world views the church as confused and double-minded.

Women in Ministry

I believe that Paul's writings were birthed by the inspiration of the Holy Spirit, even those Scriptures we consider to be hard to understand. However, much of his writing reflects historical situations that must be interpreted in context. At the same time, it is apparent that Paul is consistent in his understanding of the role of women in the church. As a proven apostle and theologian, he lays out a delicate balance of scripture that is often misinterpreted as being too complex for the average believer. Yet when all of Paul's writings are viewed in context, there is a common thread of truth that emerges!

First, Paul was not a woman-hater as some may think. In fact he commends a number of women in his epistles. In the book of Romans, he sends affectionate greetings to more than a half-dozen women of God. This list includes *Phoebe* the deaconess; *Priscilla* a fellow worker in Christ; *Mary* who labored among the church; *Tryphaena and Tryphosa*, sisters who were workers in the Lord; *the mother of Rufus* who was a mother also to Paul; *Julia* a Roman female; and the *sister of Nereus* who were counted among the saints. Paul clearly displays a fondness for women unsurpassed by the other apostles.

66

Second, **Paul encourages all, male and female, bond and free, to desire spiritual gifts, especially prophecy**. Therefore, in the realm of the gifts of the Holy Spirit there are no restraints on women as some suppose. It's true that Paul instructs the Corinthian women to keep silent in the church, but we must also understand the historical implications of this statement. In the Corinthian church, women and children were seated on one side and men were seated on the other side. Due to this seating arrangement, it is believed that the wives could not hear what was being said. As a result, they interrupted the meetings by yelling questions to their husbands who were seated across the room.

In response to this confusion, Paul had no choice but to restrict the voice of the Corinthian women. Paul's command to keep silent was not a spiritual issue but an issue of culture and order. It was never intended to be taken out of the context of his day or arbitrarily applied to diverse cultures. Nor was it to be used to devalue women in the Church then and now. Had Paul known that such abuse would occur, I'm sure he would have defined his intentions more clearly.

Third, it is believed by many that Paul draws a clear theological line between ministry function and office. Those who hold this view readily agree that women can operate in the gifts of the Spirit and flow in spiritual ministry. Yet they deny females access to the governmental offices of apostle, prophet, evangelist, pastor and teacher found in Ephesians 4:11.

Their reasoning is twofold. To begin with, they hold to the theology of male headship found in many Old and New Testament writings. The idea is that men are given leadership roles in both family and church government. Paul, himself, promotes this concept as divine order by declaring, "the head of every man is Christ; and the head of the woman is the man..." (I Cor. 11:3).

He further strengthens this chain of authority which is God-Christ-Men-Women-Children by prohibiting those who are under authority to usurp the authority of those over them. In this instance, it is the woman who is forbidden, "...to teach, or usurp authority over the man" (I Tim. 2:12). Therefore, many believe that women can freely minister under the leadership of men, but cannot lead or rule in a governmental position within the Church, especially that of apostle or prophet.

The second reason that is used to exclude women from functioning in a fivefold office is found in Eph. 4:8-11. Here Paul speaks of Christ distributing the ministry offices to the church, and writes, "He [Jesus] led captivity captive, and gave gifts unto men...He gave some, apostles; and some, prophets; and some, evangelists; and some, pastors and teachers." Many teach that when Jesus, "...gave gifts unto men," that the gifts spoken of were the office of apostle, prophet, etc. They further state that had these offices been given to both sexes, Paul would have included women in this verse instead of signifying the male as the beneficiary of the fivefold ministry.

Is it right to exclude women from the ministry offices of Ephesians chapter four? Some may think so, but I think it is important for us to maintain an open mind. We, the created, would have to agree that God, the creator, established a divine order for the role of men and women. Even so, we must also consider that some of Paul's writings were influenced by ancient custom and culture. Indeed, the historical setting in which he lived was filled with bias against women. For that reason, in all fairness to those who affirm women in ministry, we will focus more specifically on a believer in the New Testament named *Junias*.

Junias

Both in the Old and the New Testaments we see women who seem to be in conflict with the Pauline writings. Deborah, who was called a prophetess in the Old Testament, ruled over Israel as a judge and also led the army of God into battle. Sarah, who is considered to be a perfect model of submission, challenged the authority of her mate more than once. In one instance, **God**

commanded Abraham to obey Sarah's voice as if it were the word of the Lord and cast out his concubine and her son **Ishmael** (Gen. 21:9-12).

In the writings of the New Testament, we see further evidence of women with spiritual authority. In the book of Luke there was Anna, the prophetess who served God night and day in the temple. As already mentioned, Phoebe was a faithful deaconess to the church at Cenchrea. Philip the Evangelist had four daughters who were noted for their prophetic gifting. Scores of other women could also be added to the long list of ministry functions found in the early church. More specifically, there is further evidence that could possibly link the New Testament Junias to the office of apostle. Paul writes in Romans 16:7, (RSV) "Greet Andronicus and Junias, my kinsmen and my fellow prisoners; they are men of note among the apostles, and they were in Christ before me"

In the book *The Apostle Paul And Women In The Church,* Dr. Don Williams approaches Junias in this manner:

The unresolved issue is whether Junias in Greek is a masculine contraction of Junianus or the feminine of Junia. The spelling in the original language is the same for either possibility. Furthermore, the phrase they are men of note literally reads they are of note. Men is absent in the Greek, and is inserted by the translators. Thus, Paul could be referring to a woman here, quite probably a husband-wife team....This would mean that Junia is a kinsman, that is, a Jew. She is also a fellow prisoner, that is she, like Paul, had suffered incarceration for her faith in Christ. Most surprising, Junia is also an apostle, an early convert even before Paul. This has lead most commentators to render the proper name as the masculine Junias rather than Junia. While a final decision cannot be reached from the text, why must we suppose that no women could be called an apostle by Paul?

69

Only the extra-Biblical assumption that a woman could not be an apostle keeps most commentators from reading Junias as Junia. The church father Chrysostom had no such bias. He writes, "and indeed to be apostles at all is a great thing. But to be even amongst these of note, just consider what a great encomium this is! But they were of note owing to their works, to their achievements." *Oh! How great is the devotion of this woman, that she should be even counted worthy of the appellation of this apostle!* (italics mine)

Balance

In conclusion, it is obvious that Scripture can be interpreted in such a way as to support either side of the debate on women. I must confess that I have drifted between the extremes of these two opinions. However, I am convinced of three things which I consider to be absolutely clear and non-negotiable. First, women can prophesy, preach, teach, heal, evangelize, etc. There are no restrictions placed on either gender when it comes to expressing the gifting of God. (Note: preaching and teaching the Bible is not necessarily the same as functioning in the office of a teacher. Likewise, the ability to prophesy is not always an indication that we are called to the office of a prophet.)

Second, I am convinced that as a male-dominated, cold church, we desperately need to receive input from our women. The warmth, spiritual sensitivity, and nurturing instincts of women are invaluable to the family of God. As indicated, the Bible resonates with numerous examples of women who greatly contributed to the welfare of the Church.

Finally, both Simeon (male) and Anna (female) prophesied over the baby Jesus in the book of Luke. **Likewise, it will take the combined efforts of today's men and women to prophetically bring forth Christ in the end-time Church.** This is a divine pattern that we must all accept; "...I will pour out my

Spirit upon all flesh; and your sons and daughters shall prophesy..."
(Joel 2:28).

Sons And Daughters

In light of Joel's exhortation, it's obvious that adults (male and female) have the privilege to prophesy. But, can children also prophesy? To begin with, God is certainly not above speaking to us through the agency of a child. Since He has encouraged us to have the faith of little children, it is not unreasonable to expect that God could or would use small children to communicate with His adult children. Consequently, we should be alert to foster and encourage our children's prophetic giftings with an awareness that God is watching us.

There are thousands of unsuspecting parents who have spiritually gifted children. I entreat these parents to cultivate an increasing sensitivity to the Spirit of God within your child. The spiritual potential that lies within their souls may one day surprise you and could easily serve to protect you! Their strange dreams and childlike impressions may seem insignificant or frivolous at first; but in most cases, these children are prophetic in nature. If the gifting which lies within them is nurtured, God might eventually commission a prophet from within your own family.

Why should we believe that God would use the innocence, the meekness and the trusting nature of our children to establish a prophetic platform for this generation? Because, the Scripture implies that God is raising up a prophetic generation, beginning with the least among us! The Apostle Peter declared this truth in Acts 2:17. Quoting the prophet Joel, he stated, "'And it shall come to pass that in the last days,' saith God, 'I will pour out of my Spirit on all flesh; Your sons and your daughters shall prophesy.'"

There are two things in this portion of Scripture which supports our claim that God speaks through prophetic children

71

today. First, Peter indicates that a great outpouring of prophetic anointing would be unleashed in the last days. Of course, we who are alive today, make up a large part of this last day's generation." Second, he made it very clear that our sons and daughters would engage in both receiving and speaking prophetic utterances.

Is there further Biblical proof which supports the concept of prophetic children? Yes! Whereas Peter's exhortation was directed toward a *coming generation,* there were a number of prophetic children who lived in ancient Israel. Consider for a moment the life of an Old Testament boy named Samuel. In I Sam. 3:1-18, God visited Samuel at an early age and spoke to him concerning his master Eli:

> Now the boy Samuel ministered to the Lord before Eli...and while Samuel was lying down...the Lord called Samuel. And he answered, "Here am I"...Now the Lord came and stood and called as at other times "Samuel! Samuel!" And Samuel answered, "Speak, for Your servant hears"...then Eli called Samuel and said..."What is the word that the Lord spoke to you..?" Then Samuel told him everything....

The Bible provides us with several other examples where young children like Samuel encountered the prophetic. We could cite the God-given dreams of a boy named Joseph or the adventures of a young Saul who found his lost horses by heeding a prophetic word. However, in keeping with our theme which focuses upon prophetic children today, we will examine some more current examples. Hopefully, we can see that prophetic revelation is not limited to the lives of biblical characters, but is also common among children today.

Prophetic Daughters

Recently, I had a conversation with a friend of mine about the prophetic tendencies of one of his daughters. Her name is Christa.

My friend explained that Christa seems to have prior knowledge about things unknowable at the time. In some instances, she has accurately forecast the time, place, and Richter scale readings of coming earthquakes.

This all began some years ago when she dreamed about a major quake that was to hit Southern California. Now it doesn't take a prophet to predict earthquakes in California, but it is difficult to pinpoint the approximate time. Christa did just that. Within a few days of her dream, we encountered one of the strongest quakes to hit the West Coast in recent years.

If Christa's prediction was only one isolated incident, I would be inclined to dismiss her premonitions. Yet, the truth is that many of her prophetic impressions have come to pass. Just recently she had another vision about a coming earthquake that will register extremely high on the Richter scale. I have prayerfully considered her impression, not because she is a friend of the family, but because she has a prophetic gift which comes from the Lord.

Christa is just one of the thousands of children to whom God is speaking to today. In light of this, the prophetic words of Christa and others like her could have greater significance than previously realized. In fact, there are those who believe these children possess revelatory information which is directly related to such things as current world affairs, catastrophic weather changes, personal warnings, etc. I, too, am convinced that this is true.

Prophetic Sons

Roland, one of my own children, had an amazing encounter with prophetic perception. He awoke one morning with a foreboding sense that something bad was going to happen that day. He cried for a long time, begging his mother not to send him to school. Knowing that Roland loved school, my wife, Rebecca, became concerned about the source of his apprehension. All he would say was, "Please don't make me go Mom, I just feel something is wrong!"

In spite of his great reluctance to leave the house, Roland was put on the school bus by a very puzzled mother. *Was there a possibility that Roland was perceiving imminent danger*, she thought? *Did he really hear from God?* Her head told her no, but her heart said to pray for the welfare of her child. So, for a period of time she gave herself to tearful intercession.

Within an hour the bus, now fully loaded with children, overturned on a remote bridge and fell into raging flood waters. The situation was more than critical. The waters were swift and deep and the bus was beginning to sink. To further complicate matters there was no one around to hear the frantic pleas for help. It seemed that all would be lost. Yet, just in the nick of time, one of the kids managed to jump from the bus and swim to the edge of the river. He then ran to a nearby house screaming for help. As a result, a call was made to the proper authorities who immediately dispatched a rescue unit to the scene of the accident.

Due to the heroic efforts of the rescue team, none of the children suffered major injury. One by one they were pulled to safety as the bus slowly drifted downstream. When all were finally on the riverbank, the bus abruptly shifted position and sank into the depths of the swirling waters.

Although credit was given to the people involved in the rescue, we believe that the safety of those children was ensured earlier that morning. Had it not been for the prophetic warning which prompted my wife to fervent prayer, we believe that Roland and the other children would have been severely hurt or even killed. Several of the families involved in that community, upon hearing about Roland's foreboding sense and knowing Rebecca and the value she placed upon prayer and intercession, attributed this to be a miraculous intervention by God. The local newspaper reported the no-fatality accident as nothing less than a miracle.

This event (and others like it) accentuates my heartfelt belief that we must never underestimate the power of God to speak through the heart of a child. Jesus said that "...out of the mouths of babes and sucklings thou hast perfected praise" (Matt. 21:16). The prophet Isaiah underscores this thought by declaring that "...a little child shall lead them" (Isaiah 11:6). I am aware of the broader interpretation concerning these two passages of scripture, but the aforementioned application is also true. **Children have the capacity for prophetic gifting.**

Nurturing The Prophetic In Our Children

As indicated, God may choose to speak to us through the agency of a child. Therefore, we need to develop the prophetic gifting which is resident within our children. The reason is threefold. First, we have been charged in Scripture, to: "Bring up your children in the nurture and admonition of the Lord" (Eph. 6:4). Second, our lives could someday depend on a word from a prophetic child. Exodus 19:6 informs us that God has called them to be a kingdom of priests to our succeeding generations. Finally, as indicated, "out of the mouth of babes and sucklings thou hast perfected praise."

If these things are true, then what methods must we employ to nurture the prophetic within our children? Are there things we can do to enhance their latent gifts? Is there a particular procedure that will help? There are several answers to these questions and, surprisingly enough, they are extremely simple. They are outlined as follows:

1. Teach your children that God wishes to speak to them — even as children.

2. Read Scriptures to your children and tell them Bible stories pertaining to the prophetic.

3. Lay hands on your children daily, if possible, praying for the prophetic gift to be stirred within them.

4. Speak prophetically to your child's spirit — prophesying God's intent for him or her. (Joel 2:28).

5. Encourage your children to share even their simplest dream or impressions with you.

6. Teach your children to interpret their dreams in context with the symbolic implications of Scripture.

7. When possible, expose your children to valid prophetic ministry.

Exposing our children to valid prophetic ministry cannot be over emphasized. In many instances, the greater part of their prophetic gifting is received and fostered through impartation, as opposed to systematic, in-depth teaching of Scripture. Although sound biblical instruction is vital, we must remember that **more is caught than taught.** Therefore, to fulfill God's mandate for us to raise up a prophetic generation in the reverential fear and admonition of the Lord, we must not only teach them about the prophetic but, model the prophetic in front of them.

In conclusion, whether church leader or laity, male or female, child or adult, it is imperative for Christians to understand the basic role which prophecy plays within their own lives and the life of the church. When God elected to pour out His Spirit upon all flesh He had a definite prophetic purpose in mind. As a prophetic people, we must align ourselves with this purpose.

For instance, the Apostle Paul — in his writings to the Corinthian church, clearly states that the fundamental purpose of the prophetic is to impart edification, exhortation and comfort. In part II, we shall devote several chapters to the discussion of prophetic purpose. In addition, we shall also examine how the prophetic is designed to bring conviction, direction, and forthtelling to the Body of Christ.

PART TWO

Sets The Stage Regarding The Basic Purpose And Ownership Of Prophecy, And Examines How To Manage This Gift And Integrate It Into The Church

Chapter Six

BASIC PROPHETIC

To possess a gift without purpose is to waste the gift that has been given.

The same can be true of prophetic ministry. It is one thing to receive prophetic anointing and yet another to have prophetic purpose. **Just as a river needs earthen banks to direct its flow, the prophetic needs guidelines to channel its awesome force.**

Those who are maturing as prophets can easily identify with this principle of focus and purpose. When initially developing a prophetic ministry there is a season when it is seems sufficient to *just prophesy.* In the mind of an aspiring or undeveloped prophet, the actual act of speaking a prophetic word often takes precedence over whether that word is clear or scriptural.

However, when the novelty of the prophetic eventually wears thin, most are left with a deep conviction that *Without a purpose the people perish* (Proverbs 29:18 paraphrased). In time, the thrill of aimless prophecy gives way to the desire to be an accurate dispenser of God's truth. As a result, the prophet learns to minister in a focused, concise, and specific flow of prophetic utterance.

In my own experience with prophetic ministry, I have also had to deal with this issue of purpose. As indicated, in the early days of my ministry I was happy to make the transition from tongues to prophecy. However, shortly afterwards, I became content to utter poetic prophecies within the confines of Sunday services at church. I was not always sure of what I said or how it applied to the listeners, but for the most part I was happy just to release my gift. Like a runaway train off its tracks, I charged into the meetings with every ounce of prophetic strength I had. There was hardly a Sunday I didn't toot my horn and blow tons of prophetic smoke.

Eventually, it seemed that God and His people had enough of me and my gift. I was asked to cool my spiritual engines and pray for wisdom. Although I was offended, my heart bore witness to the notion that I should pull back on the, throttle for a while. After slowing down a bit and evaluating the effectiveness of my ministry, I soon realized my weakness. My prophecies were lacking in purpose and direction.

In an attempt to compensate for the lack of prophetic focus, I, along with many others, began to establish definite guidelines for prophesying. The goal was clear. We were determined to bring wild, unfocused, prophesies under control. Aimless utterances (which generated more confusion than revelation) were put to rest, no matter how poetic or spiritual they appeared to be. From that time forward, we began to focus more on the purpose of each prophecy rather than on its profundity.

At first, there were simple rules like: "Avoid utterances which are mystical and are not direct and down-to-earth...don't prophesy contrary to the spiritual flow of a service, or interrupt those who are teaching the Word...avoid prophesying to women unless their husbands are present...never embarrass people by divulging secret sins...refrain from giving directive words in a private setting...and, when possible, never use the gift of prophecy to discourage the Church."

For awhile, this prophetic protocol was sufficient; but as the Body of Christ began to grow, things became more complex. So, in an attempt to further refine prophetic ministry, we added more specific guidelines to the list. Some of these included: "Never rebuke an elder through prophecy...stay away from prophetic matchmaking, namely prophesying marriages...always use caution when predicting the birth of babies...avoid the temptation to prophesy riches to unstable sheep...and, never show partiality when delivering the Word of the Lord."

Installing these safeguards seemed to be the right thing to do at the time. If nothing else, they did bring a certain credibility to our crude beginnings. However, we seemed to focus more on what not to do, as opposed to what to do. We were negative in our approach rather than positive. Furthermore, our attempt to give structure and purpose to the prophetic was noble, but not always scriptural. The result was confusion and debate.

Many years have passed since those early days of my prophetic ministry. Yet, the questions remain the same. What is the antidote for random and unfocused prophecies? How can we bring focus to prophetic ministry? Can we connect our gift with the purpose of God and minister effectively to the Body of Christ? If so, then how do we accomplish it? Finally, where do we begin?

The answers to these questions are not as vague as some might think. **If, prophecy is a biblical gift, then the blueprint for its operation is also found in the Bible**. More specifically, these issues are clearly addressed in the New Testament, especially in Paul's letter to the Corinthian church. Therefore, in the following sections of this chapter we will examine some of the more crucial purposes of prophecy detailed in Scripture and highlight them with personal experience.

Edification

> "...he that prophesieth speaketh unto men to EDIFICATION, and exhortation, and comfort." (I Corinthians 14:3 emphasis mine).

Throughout history, the Church has been partially sustained through the power of prophetic edification. In both the Old and New Testaments, we find men of God who were built up in their faith and motivated to press forward as a result of prophetic encouragement.

Included in this list of benefactors was a weary king named David, a religious zealot named Saul (who later became Paul the Apostle), a young pastor of the early church named Timothy, and our Lord Jesus Himself. All of these were strengthened and empowered by God through prophetic words of edification (I Chron. 17:7-15, Acts 9:10-18, I Tim 1:18, Luke 2:27-33).

Although there are various other accounts of prophetic edification found in the Bible, prophetic words of encouragement are not simply relegated to the historical Church. We desperately need them in today's world of demonic oppression and social stress. For this reason Paul instructs us to, "Keep encouraging one another so that none of you is hardened by the lure of sin" (Heb. 3:13, Jerusalem Bible). In I Thess. 5:11 the apostle admonishes Christians to, "...comfort yourselves together and edify one another." In I Cor. 14:12 he writes, "Strive that you may excel in building up the church" (RSV). In Eph. 4:16, he introduces the thought that the Body of Christ is built up and encouraged "unto the edification of itself in love."

In light of Paul's writings we, as Christians, have no other option than to dispense encouragement and edification to the Body of Christ. Nevertheless, before we are proficient in this ministry there are several basic truths which are central to the concept of encouragement.

First, the Greek word *oikadome* is often translated as *edification* in the English language. In many other places in Scripture, it is rendered *building*. Thus, the words *edification* and *building* are interchangeable throughout much of the New Testament. Overall, these two words actually mean to build up, construct, confirm, establish, and improve.

Second, when the Jews referred to the building of the Temple in John 2:20, *oikadome* is used once again. Likewise, the term *oikadome* is also applied to believers who are *living stones* built up (*oikadome*) unto a habitation of the Lord. In one instance, edification denotes the construction of a natural temple. Elsewhere, it clearly indicates the building up of the saints of God.

So, in light of the need to build up the Body of Christ, Christians determined to operate in the prophetic should concentrate upon using their gift to facilitate the ministry of edification. This was made very clear to me at the beginning of my ministry. While meditating upon the priorities of the prophetic, God began to speak to me in a most unusual fashion. In a near-audible voice which seemed to penetrate my entire being, He said:

"One of the greatest ministries you can ever possess is the ministry of encouragement. In a world without hope, people need the affirmation of My love. Signs, wonders, miracles, healing and teaching are important, but are secondary to the great commission of encouragement." He continued, *"Encouragement is the motivational force behind the ministry of Jesus and should also be the priority of all Christians.* **So, bless rather than curse, build up where others have torn down, and always use your gift for the edification of mankind."**

Without a doubt this simple word from God has been indelibly imprinted on my heart. As a result, I have learned to resist the temptation to unnecessarily reprove the church. By choosing to prophesy positive words of edification, I've seen the joy of life restored to suicidal people. I've seen manic depressives completely delivered. Weary Christians at the brink of despair have been encouraged to try again. Marriages have been mended, and rebellious children have turned to the Lord. All this because a word fitly spoken accomplishes more than a rebuke out of season.

So, for those prophetic people who feel compelled to bludgeon the body of Christ with their gift, I have a few things to say. First, we must develop a deep conviction that God is <u>not</u> angry with His people. He loves them unconditionally and wants His spokesmen to speak to their hearts in a kind way. **It's true there are**

occasions when it is necessary to prophesy correction, reproof, and rebuke, but it should come as a last resort not as a first response.

Second, we are called to be body-builders not wife-beaters. So, be forewarned, when the Chief Shepherd returns, we will give an account for the stewardship of the gifts He has given us to encourage and build up His bride. Consequently, if we are abusive to the Lord's wife, we must prepare ourselves for the judgment of God against those who, in spite of their commission to edify the Church, habitually malign her.

Third, we will be judged for every harmful word that proceeds out of our mouths. "And the King will answer, 'I tell you solemnly, in so far as you did this to one of the least of these brothers of mine, you did it to Me.'" Accordingly, it behooves us to,"Let not corrupt communication proceed out of your mouth, but that which is good to the use of edifying..." (Matt 25:40, Eph. 4:29).

Exhortation

"But he that prophesieth speaketh unto men to edification, and EXHORTATION, and comfort."
(I Corinthians 14:3, emphasis mine).

The word *exhortation* is closely associated with the word *edification*. These two words denote encouragement. Though similar, there is enough difference to justify an investigation into the more specific meaning of exhortation.

Webster's Dictionary defines exhortation in this manner: "To urge or incite by strong argument, advice or appeal; to admonish earnestly." This definition is distinct from the *building up* of edification. *Strong's Concordance* verifies this distinction by rendering exhortation as, "The act of crying out, wooing and calling near." Thus, exhortation, as related to prophetic utterance, means "To prompt and urge the church to draw near to God."

I am convinced that a major part of prophetic ministry is given to help propel the church forward in Christ. True prophets do this by first discerning God's intentions for His people and then prodding them on in that general direction. Paul makes this clear to Timothy in II Tim. 4:2, instructing him to "Exhort with all long-suffering." The image is one of a shepherd who patiently leads his sheep. He doesn't angrily drive the flock but gently urges them on to greener pastures.

In the same way, prophets must gently direct the Church toward Christ. When prophetically addressing the people of God it is wise for the prophetic person to steer clear of harsh ultimatums. **Prophecies that present God as being eternally angry, intolerant, unmerciful, and ready to kill should be avoided at all cost.** Fear tactics and excessive pressure have never been the basis of biblical exhortation and never will be. God is a God of love who motivates out of love. Satan is the one who uses fear to promote his purpose.

For this reason, the Bible sets clear boundaries for exhortation. We are instructed to exhort those who are weary to "Cleave unto the Lord!" All who have not girded their minds with truth are also exhorted to be sober minded. Exhortation is also given to the prayerless Church in order that they might give themselves to supplication and prayer. And those who are discouraged are exhorted "to continue in the faith" (Acts 11:23, Tit. 2:6, I Tim. 2:1, Acts 14:22).

(Please note that I am not promoting a faint-hearted form of prophetic ministry that tolerates the indulgence of gross sin. In fact, there are times when the Lord calls us to boldly rebuke those who repeatedly resist the wooing of the Holy Spirit. Yet, when leading the flock, we must understand that it is goats who need to be pushed, not sheep).

83

Comfort

> "But he that prophesieth speaketh unto men to edification, and exhortation, and COMFORT"
> (I Cor. 14:3, emphasis mine).

Another fundamental purpose of prophetic ministry is to comfort. This characteristic is often known as consolation and its root form means to *come alongside*. Comfort also means to strengthen and to reinforce. It denotes physical, mental, and spiritual refreshment. In both the Old and New Testaments, comfort stems from the tender love of God for His people. Oftentimes, it counterbalances the troubles of life and the discouragement encountered in the work of the Lord.

To comfort the brokenhearted is a highly valued virtue in the kingdom of God. This is seen throughout much of the Bible when prophets repeatedly pronounced God's lovingkindness towards His people. Isaiah 40:1 illustrates this principle by writing, "Comfort ye, comfort ye, my people, saith the Lord." He further reveals God's intentions in Isa. 51:3 by declaring, "The Lord will comfort Zion..." When prophesying the future ministry of Jesus, Isaiah writes, "The Spirit of the Lord God is upon me; because the Lord hath anointed me...to comfort all that mourn" (Isa. 61:1,2).

In the New Testament, we are also told that God is the "God of all comfort." Jesus strengthens this truth by saying, "Blessed are they that mourn: for they shall be comforted." At the end of His earthly ministry He instructed His disciples saying, "I will not leave you comfortless" (II Cor. 1:3, Matt. 5:4, John 14:18).

Years later, the apostle Paul declares, "God will comfort us in all of our tribulations." He continued by exhorting believers to "Comfort the feeble-minded," "Comfort those that are cast down," and finally to "Comfort yourselves together" (II Cor. 1:4, I Thess. 5:14, II Cor. 7:6, I Thess. 5:11).

Considering the importance of these Scriptures, it behooves us as prophetic people to speak comfortably to the people of God. Why? We must come to realize that pronounced judgment doesn't always reach the heart of an indifferent Church. Instead, it is the goodness of God which leads to repentance. This truth is supported by the scripture, "Mercy triumphs against judgment" (Is. 40:2, James 2:13, Rom. 2:4).

Encouragement vs. Discouragement

A few years ago I was teaching this principle to a group of pastors in Melbourne, Australia. On one particular evening, we dedicated more than an hour to the issue of comfort in conjunction with prophetic utterance. After thoroughly explaining basic prophecy as edification, exhortation, and comfort, I then released the group to prophesy to each other. I instructed everyone to exclusively prophesy positive words of encouragement. My final instructions to them were, "Say nothing negative to anyone."

In spite of these instructions, someone prophesied to a young Christian that he had cancer. The frightened man who received this supposed encouragement stood in the middle of the sanctuary actually shaking like a leaf. I tried to console him, but to no avail. He left the meeting believing that he had terminal cancer. Just imagine what he might have felt! Even if he received a positive report from a doctor contradicting this negative word, he still suffered the pain resulting from undue stress and worry.

In light of this incident, it is apparent that prophetic people should focus solely on edification, exhortation, and comfort. **Unless you are a mature, proven prophet who hears clearly from God on such matters as sickness and disease, you should never discourage people with negative prophecies.** It is not only unhealthy for others but dangerous for you. There is a distinct possibility that the prophetic curses you have spoken could come back on you. Jesus said, "Judge not, that you be not judged. For with the judgment you pronounce you will be judged, and the measure you give will be the measure you get" (Matt. 7:2, RSV).

A friend of mine had an experience which illustrates this principle. Once, while ministering under a powerful anointing from God in a public meeting, my friend said some critical things about another ministry. The Lord sharply rebuked him for using his prophetic gifting, *especially under the anointing* and in a public setting, to criticize a fellow servant of Christ.

The Lord then told him that he had incurred judgment for that act and that the judgment would be one month of severe sickness and public silence for each minute of judgment (criticism of this ministry) spoken while under the anointing. The subsequent months were extremely difficult for him, with my friend facing a life-threatening illness. After the prescribed period of time, he was healed -- raised up to resume his ministry, warning us young prophetic pups to use great caution while ministering under God's anointing.

Chapter Seven

ADVANCED PROPHETIC

In the previous chapter, it was suggested that basic prophetic purpose consists of edification, exhortation, and comfort. It was further indicated that this realm of prophecy is accessible to almost anyone who wishes to encourage the church, even those who are beginners in prophecy. However, there are other areas of prophetic purpose that should be exercised only by those who are advanced in their gifting. In the following pages of this chapter we will discuss these areas of prophetic ministry which includes: conviction, impartation, direction, and foretelling (prediction).

(Note: In this chapter we have omitted the issue of correction through prophecy. This aspect of the prophetic is critical to the welfare of the church but pertains exclusively to the office of a prophet -- not to basic prophetic ministry. This issue will be explored in the latter part of this book. Therefore, we must reemphasize that **the main purpose of the prophetic is positive affirmation, not correction and rebuke**.)

Conviction

> But if all prophesy, and an unbeliever or outsider enters, he is convicted by all, he is called to account by all, the secrets of his heart are disclosed; and so, falling on his face, he will worship God and declare that God is really among you. (I Cor. 14:24-25, RSV).

As a legal term, being convicted means, *to be found guilty.* In common language it means *being persuaded or convinced.* In theology, it means being convicted at the bar of one's own conscience as a sinner in view of God's law. The means by which this conviction comes are varied. It can be imparted through preaching, reading, and hearing the Word, meditation upon

Scripture, heart reflection, or calamity. Occasionally, it comes through the prophetic.

When used to bring conviction, prophecy can be a powerful instrument in the hands of Christians. As a tool for evangelism, it is quite different from the three prophetic functions which were discussed in the last chapter. The distinction is made, not solely for the sake of protocol, but with regard to the spiritual condition of those who are addressed prophetically.

In most cases, a prophetic word of edification, exhortation, and comfort is sufficient for most believers. Usually what these Christians need is encouragement, not conviction. On the other hand, stronger measures (such as conviction through prophecy) are required to get the attention of unbelievers and backsliders. For instance, when prophetic words expose the secrets of their hearts, they are then graced with an opportunity to humble themselves, repent before God, and worship.

As indicated, it was Paul who established the validity of prophetic utterance to bring conviction upon an unbeliever. It is interesting to note, however, that these verses in 1 Cor. 14:24-25, place the unbeliever inside the meeting place as opposed to outside the church in the marketplace. Whereas this might have been the case in Paul's day, the percentage of unbelievers attending today's church is quite small.

Thus, in today's society, it would not be unreasonable to apply a reversal of this Scripture. We can take the initiative and go to the unbeliever as opposed to waiting for them to come to us. While invading their turf with the gift of prophecy, we give God the opportunity to bring conviction on their hearts by revealing intimate details of their lives.

What an incredible thought! Wouldn't it be great to walk up to a total stranger on the street and say something like this: "Hi, God loves you so much that He has revealed some specific details of

your life to me. He shows me that your name is Jim, you \
born in May of 1950, you have three children, your wife recentl_
left you and you are prepared to commit suicide."

If these things were true, don't you think that this person would
be shaken by your ability to have *read his mail* and would then
acknowledge the loving power of our omniscient Father God who
gave you such detailed and accurate information? According to
I Cor. 14: 24-25, this person would probably fall under the power
of conviction, affirm that God is with you, and begin to worship Him.

This principle of evangelism through prophetic ministry is also
found in the Gospel of John. Upon receiving a prophetic word, an
Israelite named Nathanael declared Jesus to be the Son of God.
Nathanael was not convicted by preaching, teaching, or miracles,
but as a result of the prophetic. John 1:47-49 describes the incident
as follows:

> Jesus saw Nathanael coming to Him, and said of him,
> "Behold an Israelite indeed, in whom is no guile!"
> Nathanael said to Him, "How do you know me?" Jesus
> answered and said to him, "Before Philip called you, when
> you were under the fig tree, I saw you." Nathanael
> answered and said to Him, "Rabbi, You are the Son of
> God! You are the King of Israel!" (NAS).

Why is this method of prophetic evangelism so often under-
utilized by the Church today? Several reasons come to mind.
First, most evangelical and fundamentalist churches do not believe
in the prophetic and therefore cannot emphasize its use as an
evangelistic tool. As a result, the Body of Christ is largely
untrained in the application of this gift.

Next, those churches who do believe in the prophetic, seldom
take it outside the walls of their sanctuaries. Because we lack
confidence and are undeveloped in hearing and expressing the
voice of God, we are afraid to exercise this gift in a public setting.

ng to get our needs and desires met, there is
pursue prophetic evangelism.

ve such an unhealthy desire to receive
recogni... r peers that **most believers value prophecy
only when it is ... deled on stage, in front of other Christians**.
Therefore, the use of our prophetic gifting as a tool of evangelism
is largely undeveloped and hardly ever used. Seldom do we find
believers who have the presence of mind to take their gift out of
the church and onto the streets.

However, I believe that this is going to change in the near
future. My hope is that thousands of prophetic people will flood
the marketplace and job sites, bringing conviction through the gift
of prophecy. I can almost envision a sign on the church door that
states, "Sorry, this institution is closed today; we've gone fishing
for men."

Impartation

"Do not neglect the gift you have, which was given you
by prophetic utterance when the council of elders laid their
hands upon you" (I Tim. 4:14 RSV).

In essence, the underlying principle of impartation means to
share, bestow, or dispense something that has great value and
substance. The means with which we impart something can be
likened to dispensing electrical current. For example, when
electricity is stored in a transformer it can be retained, discharged,
or sent to various places at will. The same is true of prophetic
impartation. We as believers, have the privilege to dispense God's
power to men.

However, you can only impart that which you possess. For
instance, if you have the measles and people hang around you long
enough, they will eventually catch the measles. You can tell them
a hundred times a day that you have the flu instead of the measles.

90

But, in spite of your confession, **people will catch what you have, not what you say you have.**

This principle also applies to spiritual impartation. In the aforementioned Scripture, it was a *gift* that was imparted to Timothy through prophecy and the laying on of hands. We are not certain what this gift was. But, obviously, he received a spiritual endowment which was first resident within those who ministered to him.

If you look closely at Timothy's experience, it was the elders who imparted the gift to him, not novices. Why? Because the immature generally lack the spiritual experience or stamina required to endow gifts upon the church. It's true that they are capable of impartation, but that which is imparted will often come from their soul and not from God's Holy Spirit. As a result, those who receive their ministry may walk away with a piece of the man, rather than a piece of God's Spirit.

In light of this principle, we must understand two critical points. First, only that which has been deposited in you by the Holy Spirit is worthy of being transferred. All else is hot air -- vain words which produce nothing more than false hope and confusion. Lastly, prophetic impartation is not to be exercised by beginners. This ministry is a function of advanced believers who are familiar with the dynamic of impartation.

The principle of impartation is demonstrated throughout much of the Bible. For instance, before his death, Jacob imparted various blessings to his twelve sons by the laying on of hands and prophecy. Moses, at the end of his ministry, prophesied over his servant, Joshua, and anointed him to lead Israel into the Promised Land. "The Lord said to Moses, 'Take Joshua...and lay your hand on him; and have him stand before Eleazar the priest and before all the congregation; and commission him in their sight. And you shall put some of your authority on him in order that the congregation of the sons of Israel may obey him.'" (Numbers 27:18-23, NAS). In other instances in Scripture, King David prophetically proclaimed Solomon's succession to his throne. Jesus imparted His power to the twelve disciples who, as a result, healed the sick and raised the dead.

I, too, have seen the principle of impartation at work in my own ministry. One of the most vivid examples took place at a meeting in Los Angles in the late 1980s. I was speaking at a prophetic conference when I noticed a group of four young people come through the door. Immediately, the Presence of God rose up within my spirit and prompted me to call them forth for personal ministry.

As they approached the platform I felt impressed to prophesy concerning the secrets of their hearts. One by one, God began to reveal specific details about their lives through the word of knowledge. In this instance, the prophetic word was so precise that the leader of this group fell on the floor and began to weep uncontrollably. Finally when this man had regained his composure, I laid my hands on the group and prophesied to them again. I declared that God would greatly use them, particularly in prophetic ministry

I had never seen these young people before. Furthermore, I didn't know that they were a rap, dance, and drama team that had been saved out of the Hollywood scene a few years earlier. Nor was I aware that they had little understanding of the prophetic. Nevertheless, I believed what God said and again affirmed them in their future ministries.

About a year later, I received a phone call from the pastor of a church concerning the young people I had prophesied over. He had asked this group, who called themselves *On Fire Ministries*, to speak in one of his meetings. The report he gave was absolutely astounding. Apparently, they ministered with an extremely high level of prophetic anointing. Several members of his congregation were called out by name and ministered to in a specific manner.

He further related that they had prophesied over some of his elders with an accuracy which "greatly exceeded their spiritual maturity."

The next time I saw *On Fire Ministries*, I asked the obvious question, "What happened at my friend's church the other day?" Rucky, the leader of the group, looked at me with a twinkle in his eye, and said with a smile, *"you prophesied this stuff over me and I received it as from the Lord. So, when I was ministering at the church, I could sense your prophetic anointing and just said what I thought you would say to the people."*

At first, the young man's explanation sounded a little weird. Yet, the more I thought about it, the more I realized what had taken place. The Spirit of God had used me to impart the prophetic to this group a year earlier. That which I possessed in the form of prophetic anointing was now operating in their lives. As a result of this impartation, they were able to reap the fruit of another man's anointing and ministry

Direction

These disciples warned Paul — the Holy Spirit prophesying through them — not to go on to Jerusalem....A man named Agabus, who also had the gift of prophecy...took Paul's belt, bound his own feet and hands with it and said, "The Holy Spirit declares, so shall the owner of this belt be bound by the Jews in Jerusalem and turned over to the Romans" (Acts. 21:4,10,11; The Living Bible).

Directional prophesy is one of the most vital aspects of the prophetic. Those who receive it have benefited tremendously. Those who reject it are often lost in a sea of uncertainty or, worse yet, find their lives in jeopardy.

In the case of Paul's trip to Jerusalem, the latter is true. He was told by prophetic utterance not to make this particular voyage.

93

In spite of a decision to go forward with his travel plans, he was given clear insight as to what awaited him. Eventually, things developed just as they were prophesied. Upon his arrival in Jerusalem, he was resisted by the elders, bound, chained, and subjected to many abuses.

In contrast to Paul's experience, the Bible is filled with testimonies of people who directly benefit from directional prophecy. As a result of prophetic guidance, lives have been spared from certain death, aimless men have come face to face with their destinies, nations have been delivered from bondage, kingdoms have been conquered, and great wars have been won.

In other instances, God's people have also found guidance in ordinary matters of life. In some instances it was whom to marry, what to say, and where to go. For example, Hosea was directed by God to marry Gomer, the daughter of Diblaim. Samuel was instructed to speak specific words to King Saul. Philip was told to go down to a desert place called Gaza.

Did directional prophecy cease with the death of biblical characters? Of course not. This dynamic of prophetic guidance is still in operation today. In fact, there are many contemporary Christians who hear from God on various issues, great and small. I have personally witnessed hundreds of situations in which believers' lives have been enhanced as a result of directional prophesy. They have benefited greatly on issues such as direction on how to find one's ministry, where to build a church, when to buy a house, how long to stay in one place, whom to trust, etc.

In turn, I have also heard horror stories about prophetic guidance. It seems that a number of Christians have been needlessly destroyed by so-called *directive utterances*. People were told to marry the wrong mate, divorce the right one, relocate to distant nations, invest in failing businesses, and do an assortment of other things that were not the will of God for them.

94

Yet, in my own experience, directive words which I have both received and given have been mostly profitable. One of my fondest memories concerning directive prophecy came as a result of a prophetic word given to me by a man called Brother Mitchell. Before I met this old prophet, I was in total confusion about the direction of my life. I had a young family, no money, a call to the ministry and a great desire to attend a Bible institute.

A friend who had heard about this dear old man of God insisted that we drive to his house in hopes of receiving a prophetic word. I was reluctant at first, but eventually agreed to make the trip. When we arrived, the old prophet greeted us at the door with a smile worthy of an angel. He graciously asked us into his little house and quickly arranged two old chairs for us to sit upon. What followed changed the course of my life.

Before I could sit down, this wonderful old prophet began to prophesy over me. He said, "I see a young man with a family. He has no finances, he is called to ministry and has been praying about going to Bible school." He then leaned forward, looked deep into my eyes, and said, "Son, it is not God's will at this time for you to go to Bible school. It's true you are called, but God wants to personally train you. That which He has for you to do cannot be learned at Bible school. Soon God will open a door of ministry and you will see His financial provision. So stand still and see the salvation of your God." He then smiled, opened his Bible and began to further instruct me on other issues related to my life. When he had finished, I knew that I had glimpsed the will of God for my life and ministry.

Hardly two months passed before things began to fall in line with the prophecy I had received. It became impossible for me to go to Bible school and, as a result, I was offered a position as a staff minister at a local church. From that point on, God began to develop my ministry according to the word spoken over me. And, to this day, I am still strengthened and guided by the words of a godly old man who understood the value of directional prophecy.

(Please Note: Unless you are fully developed in this gift, it is best to refrain from directive prophecy. If you are in error you will bear the responsibility and judgment which comes from sending God's sheep down the wrong path. **Remember, one of the main purposes of prophecy are exhortation, edification and comfort**

To Foretell

"...The prophets have inquired and searched diligently, who prophesied of the grace that would come unto you..." (I Peter 1:10, emphasis mine).

Foretelling is the predictive element of prophecy. Its roots are in Messianic predictions found in the Old Testament. Many old covenant prophets spoke of things yet to come, especially the earthly ministry of our Lord Jesus. It began with Moses who said, "...God will raise up unto thee a prophet [Jesus]... like unto me, unto him will you shall hearken." Isaiah and other prophets also predicted the coming of a Just One who would deliver His people. The last prophet to foretell this great event was John the Baptist. He cried, "...He [Jesus] who is coming is greater than I, whose sandals I am not worthy to carry..." (Deut. 18:15, Matt. 3:11, RSV).

In less significant matters, other prophets foretold events such as coming floods, droughts, famines, economic failures, wars, etc. Joseph correctly interpreted Pharaoh's dream, and, as a result, saved Egypt and the nation of Israel from famine. The prophet Daniel accurately forecast the rise and fall of kingdoms hundreds of years in advance and correctly interpreted the times and the seasons. John the Revelator prophesied events that would take place thousands of years after his death. Finally, Jesus, the greatest prophet of all time, gave us prophetic insight into things which transcend the life span of our globe. He prophesied future times, eons of millennia to come.

96

In much the same way, *predictive prophesy* operates in prophetic ministry today. Many present-day prophets have accurately foretold such events as the birth of babies, the election of future presidents, the fall of immoral ministries, imminent airplane crashes, coming floods, earthquakes, etc.

I, too, have seen these kinds of prophecies fulfilled in my own ministry. With the help of God, I was able to warn the church about the San Francisco earthquake of 1990. Seven days before it occurred, I released a prophetic statement detailing the time and Richter scale reading of the quake. This prophecy was spoken at Newport Beach Vineyard Christian Fellowship in Newport Beach, Ca.

Likewise, the great floods of 1993 began only a few months after God prompted me to prophesy about a great deluge of water which would bring destruction to parts of this nation by the end of the year. I prophesied this in a radio interview which was broadcast by station KTYM in Los Angeles on January 1, 1993. To the surprise of many, both of these prophesies came to pass as detailed.

As significant as they may be, these two calamities are but a few of the major events that other prophetic people have been privileged to foresee during the last few decades. In spite of this, however, many people still question God's willingness to reveal such things to His people. They just can't believe that revelation knowledge of future events are tokens of God's grace — designed to strengthen our faith in an all-knowing creator.

It's true, these tokens of revelation may not be absolutely critical for our survival today. However, in the days to come, prophetic impressions will serve as a warning to prepare us for the great calamities which are approaching Planet Earth. In fact, Scripture is replete with example after example of how God used His prophetic spokesmen to save and deliver God's people and the world.

For instance, Noah was forewarned of things to come and... "prepared an Ark for the saving of his household." Jonah prophesied over Nineveh and saved that city from imminent destruction to come. Likewise, we will also be able to deliver our families from the devastation of future calamities through prophetic prediction. Like the sons of Issachar we will have insight into the times and seasons (Heb. 11:7, I Chron. 12:32, paraphrased).

Amos 3:7 (NIV) says, *"Surely the Sovereign Lord does nothing without revealing His plan to His servants the prophets."* Thus, the issue is not whether God is willing to reveal His purpose to mankind. Rather, the issue is how do we train up this new generation of prophets to hear the voice of God and then dispense their saving knowledge to the nations? In light of this question, the subsequent chapter outlines how God uses various ways and means to dispense prophetic revelation.

Chapter Eight

HOW TO RECEIVE PROPHETIC REVELATION

No two people are exactly the same. Just as each snowflake is different in shape -- the physical, emotional and mental configuration of humans varies from person to person. **We all have the same basic design but under no circumstances do we feel, reason, act or think in the same way. Unequivocally speaking, we are unique expressions of God.**

This uniqueness is also seen in the way we respond to outward stimulus. For example, three different people might attend a musical concert and have three different reactions. The first person might find the experience uplifting because of the refreshing rhythm of the music. The second one might be irritated by the beat and volume, hearing nothing but loud noise. The third could be so touched by the words of the song that he or she are oblivious to the music. They all heard from the same source but received and responded differently.

As it is in the natural so it is in the spiritual realm. **The way in which Christians receive spiritual input varies according to the uniqueness of their personality and spiritual makeup**. God didn't create Christian clones who respond as robots to a set program. Instead, He created us divinely distinct, as independent life forms who hear from The Creator on different spiritual frequencies. Because we are unique in this reception, we have the freedom to interpret incoming revelation in a way that is compatible with our understanding.

This principle of reception and interpretation is much like radio broadcasting and receiving. According to the 1983 edition of the *Lexicon Universal Encyclopedia*, volume 16, page 44, a radio tower transmits energy in the form of radio waves. These radio waves travel at the speed of light (186,000 mi./sec) carrying specific information. When the waves arrive at a receiving antenna, a small electrical voltage is produced. After this voltage has been amplified, the original information contained in the radio waves is retrieved and presented in an understandable form. This form can be the sound which comes from a loudspeaker, a picture on a television, or a printed page from a teletype machine.

The same is true of prophetic reception. **God operates like a transmitting tower that broadcasts day and night. His Spirit is like radio waves which carry vital information. And, as believers, we are His receiving antennas awaiting a signal from heaven.** So, in most cases, whether we know it or not, we all receive prophetic transmissions from God. However, they are usually interpreted into different forms such as visions, dreams, impressions, etc. The form this information takes depends on the specific equipment within our spiritual house i.e., the frequency we are turned into and the position of our antennae.

In light of this principle, **it would be foolish to stereotype the way Christians receive from God.** We should never expect others to operate exclusively on our particular frequency. Remember, the way we interpret incoming prophetic signals is not the standard by which others should function. It just happens to be one of the many forms the infinite, omniscient, omnipresent, Almighty God communicates with His creation. Therefore, in the following pages of this chapter, we will investigate a few of the more common ways we receive revelation.

Visions

One of the ways we receive prophetic communication is through visions. The English words *vision* and *visions* are referred to over 100 times in the Old and New Testaments. The root meaning is *to perceive or see*. One Bible commentator defines a vision as "a supernatural presentation of certain scenery or circumstances to the mind of a person while awake." Another describes visions as "inspired insight of revelation from God."

100

My definition of visions is similar. I am convinced that there is a point and place in time when supernatural perception merges with natural perception. While in our conscious state, we see images superimposed over our eyesight. It is much like peering through a powerful telescope and seeing things that are undetectable by the naked eye. Some say this phenomena is enhanced by prayer and fasting. Others say that it is initiated by the sovereign will of God. Whatever position we take, one thing is certain. Like Paul, we too can "come to visions and revelations of the Lord (II Cor. 12:1).

Visions were common among many prophetic people in the Bible. In the Old Testament it is recorded that, "The Lord came unto Abram in a vision." Baalam spoke of himself as having seen "the vision of the Almighty." Samuel feared "to show Eli the vision." Isaiah referred to his writings as "the vision of Isaiah the son of Amoz." Ezekiel declared, "The Spirit took me up, and brought me in a vision by the Spirit of God." Daniel had "visions of his head upon his bed." Habakkuk was told, "Write the vision and make it plain." (Gen. 15:1; Num. 24:4; I Sam. 3:15; Is. 1:1; Eze. 11:24; Dan. 4:13; Hab. 2:2).

The New Testament informs us that Zacharias, the father of John the Baptist saw "a vision in the temple." Peter, James, and John saw a vision of Jesus standing with Moses and Elias and were told, "Tell the vision to no man." Peter related that while "in a trance I saw a vision." At Troas, "A vision appeared to Paul in the night." And lastly, John the Revelator declares, "I saw the horses in the vision." (Luke. 1:22; Mt. 17:9; Acts 11:5; Acts 16:9; Rev. 9:17)

Like their biblical counterparts, many present-day Christians have supernatural visions. It's not uncommon for them to receive visions which contain warnings, prophetic messages, predictions, and insight into the realm of heavenly things. Some have had visions of apocalyptic judgment and have seen grandiose imagery

101

of Jesus and His kingdom. Others have visions relating to the everyday affairs of life.

In my own experience, visions have played a significant role in shaping my life and ministry. One of these visions came at a very critical time in my life. Around 1985, I was desperately seeking God as to His geographical will for my family and me. There were several options open to me, but I wasn't sure which location was right. One night, while praying about this matter, I fell asleep shortly after midnight.

Three hours later, I was awakened with the sense of God's presence within the room. I immediately fell into a multi-dimensional vision. In this vision, I was physically lying in my bedroom in Arkansas while at the same time viewing the West Coast from a very high distance. Suddenly, what I discerned to be an angel came and stood at my right side and pointed to the coastline. The angel said, *"This is where God wants you. Obey God and live, disobey God and die."* These words were repeated two more times, then the vision disappeared.

Needless to say, I obeyed the vision. Not long after that night, I packed my family into our little car and headed west. I had more than 1,500 miles to travel and less than $500.00 in my pocket. And, to complicate matters, there was no church or ministry awaiting our arrival. All I possessed was my family, faith in God and the memory of a searing vision that had been etched into my brain. When we arrived in California, God began to bless us because of our obedience to the directive of this heavenly vision.

Dreams

The *Lexicon Universal Encyclopedia* (1983 edition, volume 6, page 266) describes dreams as follows:

A dream is a series of images and ideas that occur during sleep. It appears that most dreams are connected with physical states, and that their psychological origin lies mainly in the region beneath "the threshold of consciousness." A majority of these dreams seem to reflect events, thoughts and feelings of the previous day or days. Dream content, in the natural, is a dynamic mixture derived from current events and past experiences, interests and urges.

Many dreams do not convey a real message to the dreamer. As Solomon says in Ecc. 5:3, these dreams "cometh through the multitude of business." They are natural in origin and have no spiritual significance. On the other hand, there are times when dreams carry specific messages from God. These dreams are supernaturally inspired and should be interpreted and applied to our lives.

To discern between natural dreams and supernatural dreams, a simple test can be used. Does the dream provoke you to pray, seek God, etc.? Is there a sense of God's presence in the dream or right after the dream? While in the middle of dreaming are you aware that the dream is from God? Is the dream repeated over and over again? Is the dream symbolic or cryptic? Is Scripture seen or spoken in the dream? Does the dream wake you abruptly? Does the dream keep coming to mind for days or weeks? If you can say yes to one or more of these questions, there is a strong possibility your dream is inspired by the Spirit of God.

Supernatural dreams are one of the most common methods by which prophetic people receive from God. In both Old and New Testament Scriptures, we find great significance attached to certain dreams. Jacob received blessing from the Lord through a dream. Joseph was given insight into his future as a result of a dream. By the telling of a dream, Gideon's army found strength to conquer the Midianites. Daniel, who was known as an interpreter of dreams, saw future events in a number of dreams. The angel of the Lord appeared unto Joseph in a dream, telling him about the supernatural birth of Jesus. Apparently it was in a dream that the angel of God instructed Paul concerning the fate of those who were traveling with him to Rome (Gen. 28:11-15; Gen. 37:5-7; Judges 7:13; Dan. 7:1; Matt. 1:20-21; Acts 27:22-23).

As a prophetic person, I too, have been given many supernatural dreams. However, most of these dreams were not given for my own use, but for the edification of the Church. On numerous occasions, I have walked into the pulpit armed with prophetic information which I received in a dream the night before. At times, I have had foreknowledge about the flow of the meeting, the spiritual state of the leaders, and a sensitivity to the secrets of strangers who were in attendance. As a result of this dream-knowledge, I've been able to impart comfort and direction to those who were in need.

One of the clearest examples of receiving prophetic information through a dream, happened to me a few years ago. The night before I was scheduled to speak at a church in Los Angeles, I dreamed that I was already in the meeting. In the dream I was prophesying to people that I had never seen before. Suddenly, I stopped and directed my attention to a young man on the end of the fifth row. I could clearly see his features, nationality and the kind of clothes he was wearing. I paused for a moment then said to him, *"Your name is Howard and I have a message from God for you."* For the next few minutes in the dream, I prophesied concerning the secrets of his heart.

The next morning I awoke from the dream and prepared to go to the meeting. When I arrived, I was whisked to the pulpit and properly introduced. I preached for about 45 minutes and then began to minister prophetically. Suddenly, I remembered the dream. I turned and looked at the end of the fifth row. As I anticipated, the man I saw in the dream was sitting there smiling at me. He wore the same expression and the same clothes I had seen the night before. With a pounding heart, I said to him, "You don't know me, but I have already met you. Your name is Howard, stand up and receive the word of the Lord." He was stunned, and stood sobbing to hear a word from a God who knew him by name.

Intuition/Impressions

Intuition has been described as "knowledge which is arrived at spontaneously, without conscious steps of reasoning or inquiry." The expression "I have an impression from the Lord" is Christian rhetoric which is similar in meaning to intuition but different in theory and application. For many Christians, the two are synonymous. For others, they are quite different. So, in fairness to each side, we will discuss both intuition and impressions.

Throughout our lifetime, we receive thousands of intuitive thoughts. No one is exempt. Although our intuitiveness is expressed in different forms, such as a gut feeling, having a sixth sense, being suddenly aware, or just having a feeling about something, this phenomenon can be experienced by sinner and saint alike.

In most cases, people react to these intuitive impressions with statements like, "Oh, I guess that was just me," or "I wonder where that thought came from." Usually, they dismiss this gut feeling not knowing that it is often an accurate impression of things which are unknowable to them at the time.

However, others believe that our intuition is relegated to the realm of the flesh and the devil. They often warn believers of the dangers incurred when dabbling in this so-called, *forbidden power*. They are convinced that intuition, as a latent power of the soul, should forever remain dormant and undeveloped. The reasoning goes something like this:

Adam in his original state possessed a godly form of intuition; but as a result of his sin this power fell out of its spiritual sphere and fell into the realm of man's soul, a domain where Satan is believed to have access and influence. Because of our fallen state, we, as Adam's descendants, now possess a perverted form of intuition once known to creation. Therefore, the use of this fallen power is off-limits to everyone but Satan, sorcerers, and fortunetellers.

In contrast to this teaching, there are Christians who believe otherwise. They believe all things are redeemable in God. They are convinced that things lost or perverted through the fall of Adam can be restored to their original intent. By embracing the redemptive work of Jesus, the second Adam, they are convinced that intuition can also be reclaimed, sanctified and used for the Kingdom of God. This principle is stated as follows:

God gave it.

Adam lost it.

Satan perverted it.

Jesus reclaimed it at Calvary.

In relation to this principle, Titus 1:15 states that, "Unto the pure all things are pure." This is the mentality of those who no longer credit perceptive powers as being a *woman's intuition* or a kind of gut feeling. To them all the attributes of fallen man are now subject to Christ, purified, and renewed for spiritual use. They also believe that **through the process of redemption, intuition can now be used as a tool of the prophetic not a tool of the devil.** Therefore, when premonitions surface, they are prophetically interpreted and applied with the aid of the Holy Spirit. (Note: Intuitive people such as Psychics, New Agers, clairvoyants, and fortunetellers often operate in a realm of divination — not in a legitimate realm of the Holy Spirit. Therefore, it is impossible for them to have a sanctified intuition.)

Impressions/Perception

As already mentioned, the statement "I have an impression" is nothing more than contemporary Christian slang. The word *impression*, as it is currently used by Christians, is neither found in Scripture nor in the English dictionary. Therefore, under such

106

circumstances it would be more appropriate to say, "The Lord has made me aware," or, "I perceive by the Spirit of God."

Unlike the word impression, there are several places in the New Testament where the word *perceived* is used. In one instance Jesus "*perceived* in His spirit" the thoughts of the scribes. Elsewhere, when dealing with the disciples of the Pharisees, He "*perceived* their wickedness." When Peter was addressing Simon the sorcerer he said, "I *perceive* that thou art in the gall of bitterness." Paul, while sailing on a ship from Alexandria said to those on board with him, "Sirs, I *perceive* that this voyage will be with hurt and much damage" (Mk. 2:8; Matt. 22:18; Acts 8:23; Acts 27:10).

This concept of prophetic perception is a common occurrence in the lives of most prophetic people today. In my own experience, some of the most accurate information I have received has come as a result of this principle. You can call it redeemed intuition, sanctified gut feelings, or spirit awareness, but the bottom line is that God has heightened my awareness to things around me. By virtue of this, I have developed a sensitivity to the inner nudging of the Holy Spirit. This has enabled me to perceive such things as imminent danger, hidden illness, secret sins and the thoughts and intents of people's hearts. From time to time, these impressions have been helpful to both the Church and my community.

An example of this sort occurred some years ago at a supermarket where I had gone to shop for groceries. While walking past a couple of well-dressed men, I suddenly became aware of their evil intentions. In spite of their business-like appearance, I perceived they were criminals who intended to rob the store once it closed. Trusting that my prophetic perception was accurate, I took a good hard look at their features and then left the premises. The next morning the local newspaper reported that a robbery had occurred at that store. Instantly, I called the police and gave them a full description of the two men I had seen the night before. As a result, they were apprehended and charged with the crime.

Inner Voice/Audible Voice

Mental institutions are full of people who hear inner and audible voices. In some cases these voices are heard by those with brain disorders or those who have abused certain drugs. Although most medical people rarely agree with me, I also believe that many of these voices come from the realm of spiritual darkness. In certain instances, these manifestations are nothing more than evil spirits who mimic human voice and speech.

In obedience to diabolical voices, thousands of people have committed disgusting acts of violence. They have been instructed by these entities to rape, torture, murder and commit suicide. To further complicate matters, these wicked spirits often insist that their commands are the *voice of God*. Those who yield to these delusions are not only convinced that they hear from God, but occasionally believe that they, themselves, are God.

As a result of this deception, people who dare to say they have heard from God run the risk of being labeled as insane. But, contrary to the belief of some, all supernatural voices do not come from Satan. There are numerous Christians who truly hear from God and are led by His voice. **If evil spirits can speak in both inward and audible voices, then God, the Creator of all things, can most certainly speak to His people.**

Jesus substantiated this truth when He stated in John 10:27, "My sheep hear my voice." In Revelation 3:20 the Resurrected Christ again declares, "If any man hears my voice, and opens the door, I will come into him." Elsewhere in Scripture, the voice of the Lord is referred to over 125 times.

To illustrate, our ancestors Adam and Eve, "heard the voice of the Lord." God confronted the Prophet Elijah at a cave,

108

"...and behold, there came a voice unto him." Ezekiel writes of the Lord, "He cried also in my ears with a loud voice." Concerning the fate of King Nebuchadnezzar, "There fell a voice from heaven." When Jesus was baptized at the river Jordan, "There came a voice out of the cloud, saying, this is My Beloved Son!" In Stephen's sermon to the high council he says of Moses, "The voice of the Lord came unto him." At Jerusalem, Peter related his encounter with God and declared, "I heard a voice saying unto me, arise, Peter." As Paul recounts his conversion on the Damascus Road, he stated, "I heard a voice speaking unto me, and saying in the Hebrew tongue, Saul, Saul." In the Book of Revelation, John writes that he also heard, "a great voice" (Gen. 3:8; I Kings 19:13; Eze. 9:1; Dan. 4:31; Luke 9:35; Acts 7:31; Acts 11:7; Acts 26:14-15; Rev. 1:10).

As indicated, the voice of the Lord comes to Christians in two forms, inward and audible. In the Scriptures previously mentioned it was usually the latter form which was used. Those whom God spoke to in this manner seemed to hear an audible voice with their natural ears. It was not an inner sense or impression which they received, but the voice of God which was manifest in the natural realm of hearing.

Although I rarely hear God in this fashion, I know several prophetic men who do. I have a friend named Bob, who has had countless experiences of this kind. He is not crazy or weird as some may think. Rather, he is a highly sensitive prophetic person who is tuned into a spiritual frequency uncommon to most Christians. As a result, there are seasons in his life where he hears the audible voice of God on a daily basis. Many of his friends liken him to a modern-day Ezekiel.

To say the least, that which he hears is valuable beyond compare. The information given to him by God is used to instruct, rebuke, and encourage the church. More specifically, there are occasions when he is told of future events that relate to weather changes, earthquakes, politics, and economics. They usually come to pass, just as he predicts.

Bob and others like him are more of an exception than a rule. Most prophetic people today rarely hear the audible voice of God. Usually it is an inner voice that speaks as the oracle of God. To some, this inner voice is defined as God speaking through their spirits. To others it is God speaking to their minds. However, the prophet Elijah simply described it as a "still small voice" (I Kings 19:12).

No matter what your definition of inner voice is, one thing is certain: many contemporary Christians are divinely led by an *inner* nudging or *whispering* of the Holy Spirit. These inner expressions of God's voice have encouraged the downhearted, given direction to those who need guidance, and protected those who are in danger. More than once, my own life has been spared by heeding the inner voice of God.

Mental Pictures

Another common way that people receive the prophetic is through mental pictures. These pictures are much like the images seen in the subconscious mind while dreaming, yet they come while awake. They are clearer than dreams but, not as vivid as visions, lying somewhere between the realm of natural eyesight and conscious thought. Often they are referred to as *seeing with the mind's eye.*

Many times mental pictures come without warning or forethought. In the same way that a camera's eye momentarily opens to capture a particular scene, the mind's eye gives us snap shots of past, present, and future images. In a split second, things can be perceived that are unrelated to one's present state of mind. These pictures can come in Technicolor or in black and white. They can also come in clear form or in abstract images.

110

I have talked to scores of people who have experienced the phenomena of mental pictures at one time of another. In some cases, these pictures pertain to the everyday, ordinary matters of life. In other instances, they are a bit less common. For example, some people have mental pictures of unexpected guests ringing their doorbells prior to their actual arrival. They have also seen, in their mind's eye, a telephone ringing only seconds before it actually occurs. Others experience mental flashes relating to matters of greater importance -- such as imminent danger, political changes, devastating weather patterns, etc..

However, whether insignificant or important, there are dangers associated with the process of receiving and interpreting the meaning and source of mental pictures. Upon perceiving an imminent catastrophic event such as an earthquake, flood, accident, etc., what must we do with it? More importantly, can we discern its origin? Is this mental picture from God? Is it an aberration of the mind? Or is it negative imagery sent by the devil?

These answers are dependent upon understanding our spiritual position in Christ. If we truly believe that we have the mind of Christ, then we need to confidently explore the possibility that these images may have actually been given to us by God. If we are uncertain about the spiritual state of our mind, then we must disregard these images until such time that we have confidence that we are operating with the mind of Christ.

How do we know that our minds are in tune with the Spirit of God? This is something every believer must discern for themselves. In grasping for an answer to this question, I have developed an inner-sense as to whether a perception is of me or whether it's of God. Most importantly, I have come to believe that I am renewed in the spirit of my mind (Eph. 4:23). Having been washed by the water of God's Word, I have developed my senses to discern that which is good and that which is evil. Because my confidence has grown through years of meditation upon God's

111

Word, this has heightened my ability to wisely steward that which has been deposited within me.

Jesus said that it is more blessed to give than to receive. Although most Christians equate this principle with the receiving and giving of material substance, it also applies to the stewardship of the prophetic. Therefore, Christians who receive revelation by way of dreams, visions, mental imagery and the voice of God, must learn to develop and dispense that knowledge in a way which is pleasing to God.

Chapter Nine

STEWARDSHIP OVER THE PROPHETIC

There are many Christians today who aspire to prophetic ministry. Some will achieve this goal and develop a fruitful ministry, others will not. Those who fail will attempt to place the blame on either of two things: God's restraint or Satan's resistance. Occasionally, the fault may lie with heaven or hell but, as a rule, **most Christians are disqualified from ministry because of their own selfish motives, not because of God or Satan.**

Selfish Christians are consumed with an insatiable desire to be ministered unto. Like a giant sponge, many of these *bless me believers* absorb every drop of spiritual water that issues forth from the wellspring of the Church. Motivated by a "What can God do for me?" mentality, they make huge spiritual withdrawals without investing back into God's economy. As a result, the resources of the Body are depleted by high-maintenance, low-output Christians, who feel no remorse in getting all the gusto they can get.

This sort of *give me* mentality prevails over much of today's Christian community. In fact, many in our ranks are so overly focused on receiving a revelation, spiritual gift, ministry, etc., that they never really minister to others. When asked to give of their time or energy, they are not willing to respond affirmatively. When others are ministering, these sheep are the first in line to receive. They are receivers not givers — reservoirs not channels.

In contrast, Jesus, the greatest prophet of all times, said in Matt. 20:28, "The son of man came not to be ministered unto, but to minister." Such was the case of other biblical prophets who put ministry before personal comfort. For instance, Joseph was faithful to minister prophetically to a butler and a baker while rotting in the bottom of Pharaoh's prison. Jeremiah and Daniel prophesied while in captivity. Paul gave prophetic instruction to

113

several New Testament churches while bound in prison. John the Revelator wrote the great prophetic masterpiece, *The Book of Revelation*, while exiled on a lonely island.

In much the same way, most people blessed with success in ministry today understand that *It is more blessed to give than to receive*. As a result, they have ceased to look for a *word* for themselves and have become a *word* to others. They now realize that **God doesn't want to speak to you as much as he wants to speak through you**.

Giving out of Obedience

As indicated, it is imperative that we consider others before ourselves. Regardless of our own needs and desires, we must attempt to unselfishly feed and nurture the Body of Christ. Once a person has recognized this fundamental principle of giving first and receiving last, then he or she can then begin to develop a base for ministry.

In addition to the principle of giving, there are several other issues related to the establishment and development of prophetic ministry which we must examine. To begin with, you cannot give that which you do not have. Hence, it is important when ministering the prophetic to release only that which we have received from the Lord, no more and no less. Lastly, we must administer prophetic words with an attitude of obedience and faith. **We must simply obey that which God says to do and believe that He is responsible for the results.**

This principle of obedience was clearly illustrated to me some years ago. After the end of a very low-key meeting, I began to minister prophetically to a group of people who had gathered at the front of the church. There didn't seem to be much anointing present that day, but out of obedience to my calling I continued to press forward with ministry. I systematically prophesied according to the measure of faith that I possessed.

114

At the end of the prayer line, I noticed a woman who seemed anxious to receive from God. I didn't know what she needed, but the Spirit seemed to say, "Prophesy to her head." Reluctantly, I approached her thinking, *"How can I prophesy to someone's head?"* What was I to say? *You have a round head, two ears and a nose?* I must admit such a prophesy was tempting but, of course, that isn't what I said. After much consideration, I turned, pointed my finger at her head and prophesied a familiar Scripture. The prophecy went something like this: "The Lord is thy glory and the lifter of your head and He anoints your head with oil."

When I had finished the prophecy, I paused and waited for a response. Nothing seemed to happen, so, I left the room as quickly as possible. I felt dejected and discouraged, and thought that I had missed God. I went home inwardly vowing to never do that sort of thing again!

A few days later, I received a phone call from the conference coordinator. His first words were, "I want to tell you what happened the other day. The woman, whose head you prophesied over, was completely healed of a brain tumor." He went on to say that the lady had been scheduled for surgery, but after the prophecy she went to the hospital for another X-ray. Much to the surprise of her doctor, the tumor had completely disappeared.

I was bewildered by this report. I remember thinking, *How could this be? I didn't have the faith for such a miracle, nor did I understand what I had prophesied.* Then I remembered the story where Jesus turned water into wine, and suddenly it became clear. Like those at the feast, I had been faithful to do my part and the Lord had been faithful to do His part. In obedience, I had given the water of the word, and Jesus had turned it into spiritual wine.

Starting Simple

The principle of obedient giving is essential to the development of the prophetic. Yet, once we begin to flow in prophetic ministry, it is important that we do not run ahead of our gifting. **Our spiritual output should never exceed our spiritual input.** If this happens, we are well on our way to failure. Like an airplane that tries to fly around the world without adequate fuel, we will also crash if there is an attempt to stretch ourselves beyond the limits of our spiritual capacity.

Likewise, only an unwise steward would withdraw more money out of an account than has been deposited. The same can be applied to prophetic people. You must operate in proportion to what you have, not what you want to spend. If God has invested a limited amount of prophetic anointing within your spirit, then under no circumstance can you expect to operate under the anointing of Isaiah the prophet. If you do, heaven's bank will not honor your demands.

As a result of ministering beyond their means, many prophetically gifted people today are spiritually bankrupt -- God has closed their accounts. When they attempt to make a large prophetic withdrawal, the check bounces, embarrassing both themselves and the Church. Consequently, they have no choice but to humble themselves and give out what they have, not what they were hoping for. Their contribution may be small and simple, but at least it's real spiritual tender and will be honored by the bank of heaven.

I have watched this scenario played out over and over again, especially among prophetic people. For instance, many beginners in prophecy are convinced they have an anointing equivalent to that of the prophet Elijah. However, after allowing them to float upon this cloud of fantasy for awhile, God eventually clips their wings. Like falling stars, they come crashing down to earth and find themselves face to face with the real measure of their gift. This reality check is sometimes played out as follows:

You're sitting in church on Sunday morning feeling overly-spiritual. You know that you are about to prophesy because of that

116

special feeling in your gut. So when the time for corporate prophecy approaches, all your prophetic juices begin to stir. Suddenly, you go into a mental trance, envisioning what will happen next. You see yourself speaking as one of the great prophets of the Old Testament. Elijah or Elisha would be your preference but, for a Sunday morning service, Isaiah will do!

As you prepare to ascend to the lofty heights of the third heaven, you can almost feel the prophet's mantle upon your shoulders. Heaven's wind is now blowing upon your face. Coals from God's altar have touched your tongue. His word is shut up in your bones like a fire. So, with a grace fit for a king you slowly rise to utter a poetic prophecy that would inspire the likes of William Shakespeare. As you stand, the heavens begin to open like a scroll. Angels are now silent, cherubim hold their breath, and most importantly, Jesus Himself leans forward to hear the profound words that will shortly issue forth from God's divine oracle. At last, the golden moment has come. In your mind you open your mouth and begin to prophesy.

As you speak of the infinite mysteries of God, there is a sound issuing forth from your mouth like the noise of many waters. Angels now cling to their clouds, God holds onto His throne as the Church falls to the floor under the awesome power of your anointing. Finally, after quoting tons of Scripture and revealing all the secrets of the universe, you then turn around gracefully and float out of the church on a cushion of air. This is what you've envisioned prior to prophesying.

After standing to speak, something completely different begins to happen. Instead of angels singing, you hear nothing but the sound of your heart racing wildly. What you envisioned as holy oil dripping from your face is nothing more than nervous sweat. The fire that burns in your belly is more like indigestion than anointing. In spite of this you open your dry mouth hoping for the best. As you begin to prophesy, what you thought would be like the sound of thunder turns out to be a high-pitched, quivering, squeaky voice

117

that is hardly audible. The prophecy sounds something like this:
"Thus saith the Lord, aah, aah, I think that, maybe, aah, aah, possibly, aah, that God is here. Oh! and aah, , He loves you too."

Now that reality has set in, you quietly sit down, feeling humiliated and embarrassed. Your desire is to escape the minute that church is over. The essence of what you said was correct and possibly appropriate, but it just wasn't the earth-shaking prophecy you had envisioned. Nevertheless, as simple as it may have been, you gave what you had — not what you thought you had.

Sticking To The Basics

When prophesying, it's better to be simple and real rather than complex and phony. Usually, it is simple encouragement that people need, <u>not</u> heavy-duty, deep revelations about their future. In most cases, a basic affirmation of God's love and protection does more for a Christian's outlook, than all the hyper prophecies that hurtle them to the outer limits of spiritual space. Therefore, a "God loves you -- He is still with you" kind of prophecy is much more valuable than we are willing to admit. As a result of a simple prophecy, I have seen backsliders return to Christ, hopeless people saved from suicide, and countless numbers of oppressed Christians receive comfort and encouragement.

Not long ago, I heard a story which illustrates the value of *simple* prophetic words. A visitor from another country was driving a car down a U.S. highway. To reach his destination, the man had to travel on a road that was unfamiliar to him. At the beginning of his trip he had noticed a gigantic sign over the freeway that read, "Interstate 10." At first the man was confident of his direction. But after traveling for awhile, he became concerned that he might be driving down the wrong highway. The further he drove, the more anxious he became.

Finally, his fears were put to rest by reading a little sign on the side of the road that said, "You are still on Interstate 10." In relating this to a friend he said, "I really like the big signs over the freeways that tell me which way to go. But most of all, I appreciate the little signs that tell me I am still going in the right direction."

Isn't that the way it is in Christian life? In the beginning, we all need the big signs from God. As new converts, our faith in the Lord seems to be dependent upon heavy prophetic words, Technicolor visions, and spiritually inspired dreams. Yet, when the light of revelation fades with the passing of time, we learn to respect the little signs that come our way. When someone reminds us that *"I the Lord am with you always, I will never leave you nor forsake you, this is the way, walk ye in it,"* we're often so grateful that we fall on our faces thanking God for these simple words of confirmation.

Starting At The Bottom

There was a song in the 1970's that went something like this: "Everybody wants to play lead guitar for Jesus, but no one wants to back up the band." The rock gospel song continued to warn about the danger of placing immature and undeveloped Christians in the spotlight. The message of the song is *"Never assume a highly visible posture until you have first developed your gift in an inconspicuous position."*

We previously demonstrated the importance of simple prophetic words. Let us now address the need to refine our prophetic skills by starting at the bottom. For instance, you don't begin as a musician by first playing at Carnegie Hall. Neither do you start a prophetic ministry by prophesying on stage in front of the whole church. You must simply begin at the bottom and, through patience and practice, your gift will eventually make room for you.

Although this is a solid biblical principle, I've encountered countless Christians who believe otherwise. They're of the opinion

119

that God creates overnight wonders. However, that has never been God's way, nor will it ever be. **The Almighty God builds His people line upon line and precept upon precept.** After they have proven themselves faithful in small things, He then exposes them to greater visibility and enlarges the measure of their gift.

The same was true of many men in the Bible. Great heroes of the faith such as Moses, David, and Joseph began their ministries after years of secret, behind-the-scenes training. In the case of Moses, he didn't wake up one morning feeling spiritual and decide to start a signs and wonders ministry in Egypt. Neither did he waltz into Pharaoh's court like some overnight charismatic wonder, itching to show off his prophetic gift. The truth is, **Moses yielded to God's process before he wielded God's power.** The miracles that he performed came as a result of 40 long years of breaking, training, and development.

Likewise, the Psalmist David ascended to the throne of Israel only after he had spent decades practicing his gift in obscure places. In reality, he was gifted and anointed as a child, but the realization of his calling came through the process of time. He began as a lowly shepherd boy, protecting his father's sheep from wild animals. Then, as a teenager, he slew a giant named Goliath. Finally, when fully grown, he led the armies of God to countless victories. David's faithfulness to God's process made him one of the most notable warriors and kings of all times.

Joseph's life and ministry is also a timeless example of what it means to start at the bottom. Due to his prophetic gift, the young lad was cast into a well by his brothers and then sold into slavery. Later, while in Egypt, he further developed his prophetic gift at the bottom of a prison. For more than a decade he served God in obscurity, faithfully practicing his gift on fellow slaves and prisoners (Gen. 37-41).

Then, when the process of time had matured Joseph's gift, the Lord placed him in Egypt's (the world's) spotlight. Standing in

120

front of the Pharaoh, he foretold calamities and blessings that were to come upon the nation. The king was so impressed with Joseph's gifting that he made the young dreamer ruler over all the land. Consequently, like Moses and David, **Joseph's ministry flourished from his willingness to be faithful in the small things — beginning at the bottom.**

The Process of Development

In conclusion, the references made to Moses, David, and Joseph are vital examples designed to counterbalance the impatience nature, characteristic of contemporary Christians. **In an age of instant everything, we have developed a Christian culture which relies on immediacy rather than intimacy.** (As a result, we have birthed a generation of push-button Pentecostals, microwave Methodists, buffet Baptists, right-now Nazarenes, precooked Catholics, presto Presbyterians, lightening-quick Lutherans, and quick-fix Charismatics.) Like impatient children with a drive-thru mentality, we want it all and we want it right now.

Perhaps in our rush and confusion we have failed to comprehend the words of a wise man, who said in Ecc. 3:1, "For everything there is a season, and a time for every purpose under the heaven." We have forgotten that we live in a realm where trees are grown, fruit is matured in its season, and babies develop according to the process of time. So to those who have received spiritual gifting, especially prophetic gifting, several things are important.

First, there is a process of development which we must all endure. In order to mature our gifting, we must be subject to God's time and seasons. While in this formative process, we must not become impatient and despise that which God has planted in us. Otherwise, we will be like the unwise farmer who angrily cut down his apple trees just because the little green apples were sour to the taste. He didn't understand that the apples were perfect in their

121

season and would one day develop into juicy red apples. He saw only the immature state of the fruit, not its potential for the future.

Second**, when God is developing our gift we must not minister beyond the level of our maturity.** We must be willing to operate with the measure of grace God has given us in simple ways and in obscure places. If we're not ready to stand before kings then, like Joseph, we must continue to practice our gift at the bottom of the prison. We must be faithful to minister, as he did, to the butlers and bakers of our day.

Last, if we could learn to be patient while in the growth process, things would be much easier for us and for the Church. We would feel less compelled to minister in front of a congregation or to prophesy over notable people. We would realize that our ministry is not confined or restricted to our Sunday church services and that, once church is over, there are still six days left in each week in which we can minister at our jobs and in the marketplace. As we use our prophetic gift to encourage those in the highways and the byways, our ministries would flourish greatly.

However, this isn't to say that we should refrain from ministry in the Church. As previously indicated, the gift of prophecy plays a vital role in the everyday life of a local church fellowship. So, in light of this, we shall explore how to relate and submit our prophetic gifting to the Church and its leadership in the next chapter.

Chapter Ten

RELATING TO THE CHURCH

It has been said that a picture is worth a thousand words. Recently, while thumbing through a Christian magazine, I came across a cartoon that clearly expressed a major problem within the Church. In this cartoon a lamb and a shepherd were squared off, face to face, ready to enter mortal combat with one another. The lamb wore boxing gloves and was standing erect on his hind legs with both hands raised in defiance.

Towering over the lamb was an angry shepherd who had his staff drawn back in a combat position, much like that of a samurai warrior. Although both seemed reluctant to start the fight, it was apparent that each one was capable of defending himself from the advances of the other. The caption over the picture should have read, "Go ahead — I dare you to hit me first."

This cartoon reflects the present conflict which exists between prophetic sheep and pastoral leadership. Only deliberate ignorance would prevent anyone from admitting that a serious breach has developed between these two groups. So great is this breach that most prophetic people avoid pastors as though they had the plague. Likewise, most pastors are relieved when prophetic people leave their churches.

Why has this breach festered into an almost incurable wound? On the one hand, the pastor feels offended because the prophetic person is reluctant to come under church authority. On the other hand, the prophetic person feels threatened by harsh treatment which he interprets as a pastor's over-controlling abuse of authority. The result is a relational standoff, a no-win situation for either side.

123

As one who has pastored several churches and traveled in an itinerant prophetic ministry, I understand the inner fears of both sides. For the pastor who is committed to scriptural balance, moderation, body life, biblical submission, etc., it is extremely hard to embrace a prophetic person who seems extreme in his revelation, mystical, free-spirited, exclusive, and independent.

For the prophetic person who feels an obligation to protect his ministry, it is equally hard to submit himself or his gift to the jurisdiction of pastoral oversight. Especially if the pastor appears to be intolerant, unapproachable, and skeptical of the prophetic. Consequently, both feel rejected by the other, making it difficult to maintain a working relationship.

Identifying Valid Prophetic Ministry

Before there can be a healing of the breach between the prophetic and pastoral ministries, there must first be an understanding of the roles played by each party. If ignorance is the breeding ground for misunderstanding and division, then both sides must educate themselves as to what Scripture says about the other. The prophetic person must understand the dynamics of pastoral function, and the pastor must understand the dynamics of the prophetic. Most important, both must recognize the role of the other as <u>vital</u> to the Church.

However, in keeping with the theme of this book, which deals solely with the prophetic, we will not attempt to explore the function of the pastoral office. Our concern is strictly related to the role and operation of prophetic ministry within the Body of Christ. Therefore, to define this ministry and its relationship to the Church, we must divide the prophetic into the following four levels:

1. The spirit of prophecy

2. The gift of prophecy

3. The prophetic mantle

4. The office of prophet

The first level, pertaining to the spirit of prophecy, is the most common form of prophetic utterance within the Church. According to Rev. 19:10 this manifestation of prophecy is the same as the testimony of Jesus Christ. In specific terms it is an anointing of the Holy Spirit which enables people who are not prophets or who do not possess a prophetic gift to prophesy. When this form of prophetic anointing falls upon a group of people, even backsliders and lukewarm Christians have been known to prophesy with great inspiration.

> ...And when they saw the company of prophets prophesying, and Samuel standing as head over them, the Spirit of God came upon the messengers of Saul, and they prophesied. When it was told Saul, he sent other messengers, and they also prophesied. Saul sent messengers again the third time, and *they also prophesied.* Then he himself went to Ramah....And, the Spirit of God came upon him also, and as he went, he prophesied until he came to Naioth in Ramah (I Sam 19:20-23, emphasis mine).

The second level, the gift of prophecy, is also fairly common to today's church. Unlike the spirit of prophecy, which falls upon whole congregations, this manifestation of prophecy is limited to a lesser number of people. As indicated in Chapter four, it is one of the nine gifts of the Spirit found in I Cor. 12 and is given by the Spirit "to whomever He wills." As previously mentioned, **the gift of prophesy is a resident gift and can be utilized at any time by those who are developed in their gifting.**

> "...Philip the Evangelist, one of the first seven deacons. He had four unmarried daughters who had the gift of prophecy. During our stay of several days a man named Agabus, who also had *the gift of prophecy,* arrived from

Judea and visited us. He took Paul's belt, bound his own feet and hands with it and said, 'The Holy Spirit declares...'" (Acts 21:8-11, The Living Bible, emphasis mine).

The third level speaks of a prophetic mantle. It is a ministry function empowered by a strong prophetic anointing that rests upon an individual at all times. It far exceeds the first two levels in commitment and calling. In commitment it requires a lifestyle devoted to the prophetic. In calling, it is often times preparatory for those who will later function as mature prophets. Much like Elisha, who received the mantle of the prophet Elijah, this prophetic mantle can fall upon a person who is in close association with a prophet or group of prophets.

"So he [Elijah] departed from there, and found Elisha the son of Shaphat, who was plowing with twelve yoke of oxen...Elijah passed by him and *cast his mantle* upon him. And he left the oxen and ran after Elijah...they said, the spirit of Elijah rests on Elisha" (I Kings 19:19 and II Kings 2:15 RSV, emphasis mine).

The fourth level embodies the office of a prophet. It is the highest realm of the prophetic. To possess the office of a prophet, one requires a sovereign calling, extensive training, and multiple encounters with the presence of God. Unlike the other levels of the prophetic, the prophet operates in a governmental office, directing and correcting the Church. He lives in a realm of forth-telling, rebuke, affirmation, revelation, illumination, prophetic utterance, prediction, encouragement, dreams, visions, correction and ministry confirmation.

"So He has given some to be apostles, others to be *prophets:* Some to be evangelists and others to be pastors and teachers, to equip the saints for the task of ministering toward the building up of the body of Christ... And God has appointed in the church first, apostles, next *prophets*...And are built upon the foundation of the apostles and *prophets,*

126

Jesus Christ Himself being the chief corner stone" (Eph. 4:11-12, Modern Language Bible; I Cor. 12:28, Modern Language Bible; Eph. 2:20, emphasis mine).

In summary, there are several points concerning these four levels of prophetic ministry which must be clarified. First, any Christian can prophesy in a level one anointing when the spirit of prophecy falls on a congregation. Second, levels one, two, and three are strictly for the encouragement, edification, and exhortation of the church. Third, the level two gift of prophecy and the level three prophetic mantle can be utilized by other ministries such as pastors, teachers, evangelist, etc. Fourth, the fact that you operate with a level two gift of prophecy, doesn't make you a level four prophet. Finally, only the level four prophet has the latitude and the authority to direct and correct the church.

Relating to Authority

When Jesus was asked to come and heal the servant of a certain centurion, the centurion said to Jesus, "Just speak a word from where you are, and my servant boy will be healed. I know because I am under the authority of my superior officers, and I have authority over my men. I only need to say, Go! and they go...so just say, 'Be healed.' and my servant will be healed" (Luke 7:6-8, The Living Bible).

When you are responsible for someone, you must also be responsible to someone. Thus, to have authority, you must be under authority. The same applies to any person or ministry in today's Church. Whether it be pastor or prophet, church secretary or worship leader, all who labor in the Lord must defer to a higher authority than themselves. This act of submission places a believer in a flow of divine order.

There are many Christians who wrestle with the issue of submission. Nevertheless, God's order of authority is clear. First, we must be submitted to God. Second, we must submit to those

127

whom God has placed over us. Finally, we must show an attitude of submission toward our peers. Scripture describes this dynamic as, "submitting yourselves one to another in the fear of God" (Eph. 5:21).

This brings up the issue of prophets submitting to authority. Have divinely called prophets erred in the areas of authority and submission? And, if so, is there a safeguard against them falling into what some would describe as a spirit of individualism and independence?

It has been said that, "No person is an island unto himself." If this is true, then all Christians are part of the larger picture. For those who are prophetic, this bigger picture is the local church. In the same way that the New Testament prophets were church-based, prophetic people must also be accountable to the authority structure God has established. Without this connection, we are in danger of becoming isolated lone-rangers, and are prone to develop into renegade prophets who answer to none but ourselves. This applies to all prophetic ministry (Acts 13:2 and 15:22).

Prophets and Submission

In the last few years, the words *submission and authority* have become nasty language for most believers. When dealing with the prophetic there is even greater contention over whom the prophet should be submitted to, if anyone. A number of Christians believe the prophet is autonomous and answers to no one but God. Some say that the prophet must be under the authority of a seasoned apostle. Yet, others declare that the prophet's ministry is subordinate to the pastor of the church where he attends or ministers. (Note: I'm not referring to those who are just prophetic or who have the gift of prophecy, but solely to those who function in the office of prophet.)

Which of these opinions is correct? Are there instances where all these concepts apply? Perhaps, but because the emphasis of this chapter concerns the breach between prophet and pastor, I will only comment on the issue of submission to the pastor. In my opinion, the prophet, himself, is not under any scriptural obligation to subject his ministry to pastors, in general. Other than submitting to the pastor whom he relates to on a frequent basis (such as the pastor of the church where he is based or a pastor to whom he is connected in a covenant relationship), he is free to conduct his life under the guidance of the Holy Spirit.

On the other hand, when ministering in a local church setting, there are many occasions when the prophet must submit his ministry to the pastor of that church. For example, when a prophet enters a pastor's domain, such as his church or parish, he has stepped out of his own realm of authority and has become subject to the authority of that pastor.

From the time he enters the church meeting until he leaves, the prophet must be sensitive to the pastor's authority over that congregation. Unless the pastor fully releases his governmental rights to the prophet, the prophet is limited in doing only that which is allowed by the pastor. If the prophet attempts to minister contrary to the limitations set by the pastor, he is in direct violation of spiritual authority. Therefore, the prophet has three choices. He must submit himself to the wishes of that particular pastor, go to another church where he is fully accepted and released to minister, or conduct his meetings in a place other than a local church.

The Pastor's Role

Now let's speak, by way of analogy, to prophets who might not understand a pastor's right of authority in his own church. The position which a pastor holds in his church is much like the position held by the head of a household. Both have the authority to regulate, establish protocol, set boundaries, etc. In light of this, which of you would enter a man's house and attempt to do as you please? None, I'm sure. If the head of the house requested that you take off your shoes before entering, then out of respect, you would comply. If he said dinner would be served at five o'clock, then you would come to the table at five not six. The rules might seem unnecessary or even silly, but nevertheless they are the rules of that house. Right or wrong, he is the head of his home and he deserves respect from those who enter his domain.

The same is true of a church and its pastor. While in his sanctuary, you come under his authority. If the pastor doesn't want you to lay hands on people, then don't lay hands on people. When he restricts you from prophesying then, don't prophesy. If he gives you thirty minutes to speak, then take thirty not forty. **Remember, it is better to submit to Godly authority than to undermine authority.**

Finally, if you feel that, as a prophet, you cannot comply with the rules, then don't hang around to complain or cause trouble. Instead, go privately to the pastor and if appropriate, kindly inform him that under the present circumstances you're unable to return and minister prophetically in his church. Then ask God to lead you to a church that is more compatible with your ministry. Pray that you will be hooked up with a pastor who understands your prophetic ministry and is sympathetic to your methods, doctrine, ministry style, etc.

(Note: The same applies to those who have a prophetic gift or prophetic mantle. If your church doesn't encourage prophetic ministry, don't push the issue. Either stay and pray that God will change things, or speak with the pastor and ask his blessing to find another church that is more favorable to the prophetic.)

A Prophet's Metron

"But we will not boast of things without our measure, but according to the measure of the rule which God hath distributed to us...For we stretch not ourselves beyond our measure" (II Cor. 10:13-14).

Metron is the Greek word for measure. It means portion or degree. In this instance of Scripture, it refers to the apostle's rule, but it can also be applied to a prophet's degree of rule, domain, or authority. In any case, the word metron can be used in a positive sense revealing the measure of one's authority. In a negative sense, it can also reveal the limitations of that authority.

In the level four office of a prophet, there are two different metrons of a prophet's rule. One is *local rule,* the other is *trans-local rule.* A prophet who has been given local rule is one who has authority in a church or churches within his city. His realm of influence is limited to a local level. He works in concert with others to build up the city church. Since he is submitted to local eldership and rarely goes outside his area to minister, he is known by some as an in-house prophet.

The trans-local prophet has either national or global influence. He is called to the Church at large, and like the apostle Paul, he travels from city to city in an attempt to encourage and strengthen the corporate Body of Christ. His vision is broader, his authority is weightier, and his anointing is usually different than that of the local prophet. He, too, is submitted to eldership. Nevertheless, he has more of a pioneering spirit, which enables him to move from region to region. His metron is only limited by an occasional restriction of the Holy Spirit, such as Paul experienced when he attempted to go into Asia:

"As they visited one town after another, they passed on the decisions reached by the apostles and elders in Jerusalem, with instructions to respect them. So the church grew strong in the faith, as well as growing daily in numbers. They traveled through Phrygia and the Galatian country, having been told 'not to preach the Word in Asia'" (Acts 16:4-6, Jerusalem Bible).

Out of Your Metron

Most contemporary prophets believe that their metron stretches as far as their airplane tickets. At times, this may be true for trans-local prophets; but for local prophets, it's dangerous to go where you haven't been called. Any attempt to minister in an area that you haven't been graced or equipped for can subject you to the attack of territorial spirits in that region. You could be hit with great temptation, physical and mental fatigue, depression, sickness, or even death (I Kings 13).

In light of these things, those who are level four prophets must determine how and where they will relate to the Church. If you are a local prophet, then stay home and support the pastors in your city. Give your attention to the building up of the local church. Focus on the needs around you, not the needs around the world. If you are a trans-local prophet, then establish a network of relationships with elders of various regions. Make sure that you work in harmony with God's global purpose for the whole Body of Christ. Endeavor to excel in the edifying of the whole church instead of settling into the comfort zone of only one congregation.

Prophet/Pastor

There is a new breed of ministry emerging in the 1990's. I call it *prophetic pastors*. It appears that in many situations God is placing prophets in the pastor's or associate pastor's position. This phenomenon may be short-lived, but for a time, the church will have to submit to it as an unprecedented work of the Holy Spirit.

Why would God allow a season in which prophets pastor the church? The answer is threefold. First, Jesus is still the Head of His church, and can make any adjustment He so desires. If He wishes to set a prophet in a church as pastor, who are we to say otherwise? (We don't seem to mind when an evangelist or teacher holds a pastoral position.) Second, because supernatural ministry has been stifled by a number of traditional pastors, the Church is in need of a prophetic shot in the arm. To do this, it will take a concentrated effort from those who live and breath, the prophetic.

Finally, but most importantly, many insensitive and unloving prophets need to be dipped into the deep waters of pastoral responsibility. They need to understand the incredible task of overseeing a church. They also need an introduction to the finer points of pastoring such as: counseling floundering marriages, comforting those in distress, discerning the wolves, protecting the lambs, feeding the sheep, marrying the young, burying the dead, rebuking the disobedient, encouraging the faithful, etc. In addition, they can benefit from the experience of being a spiritual father, mother, priest, teacher, midwife, policeman, and general problem solver.

Give a prophet six months of pastoring, and I assure you he will have a different attitude towards pastors. The next time he enters a pastor's church, compassion and empathy will ooze out of him like honey from a honeycomb. He will not be so apt to do his own thing. He will have developed an empathetic heart to accommodate the pastor in any way possible.

(Please note, God doesn't have a problem with the many wonderful and gifted pastors who are striving to bring their sheep into the realm of the supernatural. These shepherds are to be commended for their courage and determination to fulfill God's mandate to equip the saints. However, the Lord is contending with those pastors who, like the Pharisees, "...shut up the Kingdom of heaven in men's faces, neither going in yourselves nor allowing others to go in, who want to" (Matt. 23:13 Jerusalem Bible).

Concluding Thoughts

In conclusion, relating to the church as a prophetic person can be both complex and frustrating at times. Regardless of this problem, an attempt must be made by both sides to reconcile the issues. As stated, we, who are prophetic, must learn how to relate to pastoral authority and to work within the boundaries set up for us. We must know our limitations and not transgress our measure of rule (this relates to all four levels of Prophetic Ministry). We must also develop an attitude of submission to pastoral authority. This minimizes the risk of becoming independent and self-promoting.

On the other hand, those who have authority within the local Church must open their hearts to the work of the Holy Spirit that is expressed through prophetic people. They must create an atmosphere of acceptance and make allowance for the mistakes, failures, and oftentimes strange behavior of immature prophetic people within their church.

PART THREE

Deals With Failure And Success;

Mature And Immature Prophetic Ministry;

And Answers The Forty Commonly

Asked Questions Regarding The Prophetic

Chapter Eleven

PROPHETIC FAILURE

The word failure has many negative connotations. For most people it means to be insufficient, unsuccessful, to fall short, to stop operating. It also implies that the person who fails does so because they are weak, faulty, imperfect, or immature. Therefore, no one aspires to be a failure.

In spite of our reluctance to admit it, failure is a reality of life that must be reckoned with. Sooner or later failure knocks on everyone's door. When failure comes, we have several choices. We can attempt to ignore it, hide from it, run from it -- or we can face failure head on and use it as a stepping-stone to success.

Depending on your attitude, failure can either be a friend or an enemy. As an enemy, it can serve as a fatal end to your dreams -- as a friend, it can become a launching pad to God's blessing in your life. Hence, you can serve failure, or failure can serve you. The choice is yours.

Failing does not make you a failure. In most cases, failure is only an opportunity to try again. This was the philosophy of a wise king named Solomon. In Proverbs 24:16, he wrote: "For a righteous man falls seven times, and rises again." Notice, he called the Proverbs 24 man *righteous,* not because he was without failure, but because he was willing to rise out of his failure.

People who have succeeded in life usually began as failures. This is especially true of many biblical characters. *Joseph* was made ruler in Egypt after years of rejection and false imprisonment. *Moses* delivered a whole nation from bondage after he had failed miserably in a previous attempt. *Rahab* was a harlot before she hid the spies Joshua sent into Jericho. *Ruth* suffered the

135

loss of her husband, family, and people before she was redeemed by Boaz and gave birth to David's grandfather, Obed.

David became one of the most beloved kings of all times in spite of moral failures such as adultery and murder. *Bathsheba* who had an adulterous affair with David, lost their first child and then sired Solomon the wisest man on earth. *Esther* was an orphaned captive who became a queen and a deliverer of her people. *Peter* was given the commission to feed and care for the Church shortly after he had denied Christ. And, *Paul*, who many acknowledge to be one of the greatest apostles of the New Testament, was initially known for his zeal in killing Christians.

Contrary to popular belief, those listed above are but a few of the biblical characters who refused to be intimidated by their failures. After failing repeatedly, most of them repented, arose from their despair, shook off the condemnation, and proceeded to be all that God had purposed for them to be. They treated failure as a temporary setback, not as an excuse to quit trying.

Fear of Failure

There are three kinds of people on the road to success. Those who fail and never try again. Those who fail but keep on trying until they succeed. And those who neither fail nor succeed, because they are afraid to try. Of the three, the latter is the worst. This person is crippled, not by failure, but by the fear of failure. He has not learned that, *"It is better to have tried and failed, than to fail by not trying"* (Anonymous).

The same is true of prophetic ministry today. I have seen scores of Christians who desire to flow in the prophetic, but who are afraid to try. Due to an irrational fear of being wrong or making a mistake, most of their life is spent dreaming about prophecy rather than appropriating the prophetic gift within them. These Christians fail to prophesy, not for lack of desire, but because they cling to an Old Testament mentality which demands that a prophet be stoned to death if he makes even the slightest error in his prophecy. Therefore, out of fear they refrain from speaking the Word of the Lord.

Yet, the beauty of New Testament Christianity is rooted in the concept that we are no longer under the judgment of Old Testament law. Unlike our Old Testament counterparts, who were often killed for their failures, we as contemporary Christians have been given New Testament grace to grow and mature through a process of trial and error. The writer of Hebrews 5:13 makes this clear, by stating that mature Christians are those who have had their faculties trained by reason of use. The implication is, that we, as New Testament believers, mature through a process of exercise and practice of our gifts.

In the same manner, today's Christian also has the liberty to practice prophecy without the fear of being stoned or judged harshly by the Church. Therefore, for believers who desire to prophesy, remember three things: **First, any voice that tells you there is no room for failure in your Christian experience, is not the voice of God. Second, you will never succeed in God unless you are willing to fail in front of your peers.** And last, instead of being crippled by the fear of failure, get up and try again and again until you get it right.

(Note: When learning to prophesy by trial and error, prophecy should be limited strictly to the realm of edification, exhortation, and comfort. When prophesying ministry confirmation, direction, correction, etc., this method of trial and error must not be used. A mistake in one of these categories of prophecy could be devastating to the person or to the church who receives your prophetic word.)

Admitting Failure

Unlike the believers just described, there are a number of prophetic people who do not fear failure. Yet when this particular group of Christians do fail, they are usually reluctant to admit it. It seems they will do almost anything to cover their misguided prophecies. They will lie, twist words, manipulate circumstances, and even attempt to blame God for their mistakes. When that doesn't work, the blame is then shifted to the person receiving the prophecy. The other person is told, "If you just had enough faith, my prophecy would have come to pass in your life."

A few years ago, I witnessed a classic case of prophetic failure which was compounded by denial. A certain prophet who was ministering to a young married couple prophesied that they would have a baby boy. Shortly afterwards the wife conceived and eventually gave birth. But, to the surprise of everyone, the baby was a girl. When the prophet was confronted about his prophecy he replied, "Hey, if you would have had faith in my prophecy, the baby would have been a boy instead of a girl." It seemed the prophet wanted credit for prophesying the baby's birth, but was unwilling to admit that he had failed in predicting the gender.

Another example of a believer refusing to admit his error occurred in a meeting where I was asked to train people how to flow in the prophetic. I had called a young man forth and asked him if he had a prophetic word for anyone. He pointed to a lady and said, "God shows me you have a pain in your left toe." She replied, "No, actually I have a pain in my head." He hesitated for a minute and said, "That maybe true, but God shows me that the pain starts in your toe, goes up your leg, through your shoulder, around your neck, and into your head."

Now there's nothing wrong with an honest mistake. Like the prophet or the young man in the examples above, we have all missed it now and then. However, an honest mistake must be followed by an honest apology. What the prophet should have said was, "I sensed you were going to conceive a child but I failed to perceive the sex of your baby." Likewise, the young man could have said, "I'm sorry lady, I believe God told me that you were in pain, but evidently I was mistaken about the location of your pain."

Had both of these men been honest, I'm sure God would have honored their integrity with an greater measure of prophetic anointing. Chances are, the next time they gave a prophecy the results would have been more favorable, greatly reducing their margin of error. For, "God resists the proud and gives grace to the humble" (I Peter 5:5, Paraphrased).

When Prophecy Fails

There are a number of reasons for the occurrence of inaccurate prophecies. The problem is usually related to inexperience, pride, or presumption on the behalf of the one who prophesies. These things greatly impact the purity of a prophetic word and are common to people who are immature. However, there are times when incorrect words are also given by some of the most seasoned prophets. For no apparent reason, these prophets seem to occasionally miss the mark, much like a gun that misfires periodically.

What is the reason for this inconsistency? Why do well-developed prophets give birth to prophetic duds now and then? Is there a safeguard against wayward prophecies? If so, then what method can we employ to consistently deliver accurate prophecies? The answer lies in a three-fold dynamic we will classify as prophetic protocol. Failed prophecy is due to an error made in one of these three areas. Let me explain!

From the conception of a prophetic word to its delivery, there are three basic stages of development. These stages are: revelation, interpretation, and application. All three are connected in sequential order and must be used in the same way. If you isolate one of these stages from the other in an attempt to shortcut prophetic procedure, the result could be devastating. Therefore, gaining an understanding of these stages and the way they are handled is fundamental to the success of any prophecy. For this reason, in the following pages, we will examine this procedure and attempt to explain how it relates to the success or failure of prophecy.

139

Revelation

Revelation is the first stage in the development of a prophecy. This is where initial contact is made with the spirit world, and as a result prophetic information is obtained. This information is most commonly known as a *Rhema word* or *specific revelation.* As previously indicated, the information can come in many different forms such as dreams, visions, inner-quickening, inner-voice, etc.

However, the problem of receiving revelation, in any form, is discerning its origin. This is where a number of undeveloped and immature prophets are prone to make an error in judgment. Due to their sensitivity and openness to revelatory communication, they are also (at times) subject to input from sources other than God's Spirit. These sources can include the spirit of man, human imagination, soulish impressions, or even familiar spirits.

For instance, **the prophetic person has a peculiar capability, an unusual receptivity which heightens his or her capacity to receive revelation from God.** However, there are occasions when revelation is mixed with information from the other sources we have mentioned. Much like a radio that occasionally picks up two different stations on one channel, people who have not fine-tuned their gift can receive a mixture of information. Therefore, extreme caution must be used when receiving revelation that is to be translated into prophecy. We must ask the question: Is it wholly God? Is it the result of an overactive imagination? Is it input from a familiar spirit? Or, is it a mixture of one or more of these things?

With regard to these questions, I had an experience as a young man that is typical of discerning the origin of revelation. While thinking about a particular member of my family, I saw a mental picture of what appeared to be an angel. This supposed *holy angel* began to speak to me about a family member. In a near audible voice, he said, "Your relative is going to fall sick and die within three days." As quick as the mental vision came, it also disappeared.

Although I did not doubt the reality of this visitation, I was left with the difficult task of discerning its source. Was it from God or was it from an alternate source? As I began to pray about the matter, I felt an inner witness that the revelation was not from God. Furthermore, it seemed that I was to consider the visitation as a powerless threat from an *angel of light*.

Three days passed and much to my relief, the revelation had proven to be inaccurate (as I had anticipated). In fact, fifteen years have passed and the person who was supposed to die is still living. Yet, for the sake of all parties involved, I'm glad I was able to properly discern the revelation. Had I spoken this word as a prophetic utterance, the error would have unnecessarily frightened my family and jeopardized the integrity of my prophetic ministry.

Interpretation

Interpretation is the second stage in the development of prophecy. After you have determined that the source of your revelation is God, you must then interpret it's meaning. This step in your procedure cannot be ignored. Proper interpretation of your prophecy is just as important as discerning the origin. Therefore, before speaking a revelation, we must ask ourselves the following questions. How does the revelation apply to the person I am ministering to? Can I give an interpretation that is relevant to their situation? Do I interpret my revelation at face value or is it a coded or cryptic message which has several different meanings? These questions are especially important for the prophetic person whose revelation comes in symbolic form.

For example, if you see a vision of a candle over someone's head how would you interpret this? Does it mean the person works at a candle factory, that they are the light of Christ, or that it's their birthday? If you have an impression that someone has no shoes, what does it mean? Does God want them to be blessed with a new pair of shoes, are their feet ready to be "shod with the gospel of

141

peace," or are they standing on holy ground, spiritually barefoot, like Moses at the burning bush?

This is where many prophetic people have missed it. In the two examples listed above, any one of the interpretations could have applied. Therefore, the proper interpretation could depend upon the circumstances of the individual and, most important, the purposes of God for that person. Thus, to make accurate interpretations we need to exercise patience and common sense. We also need a great measure of God's grace.

I want to cite another example which illustrates the necessity of coupling revelation with proper interpretation. One evening after a Bible study, I was asked to minister to a lady who was having severe emotional problems. We will call her Mary. Touched by Mary's plea for help, I immediately began to pray about her situation. Halfway through my prayer, I had a vision of a broom lying beside Mary. I was certain the revelation came from God, but I was unsure of the interpretation. So, in my mind I began to ask myself several questions.

Did God want to sweep Mary's past away, I mused? *Or, had she been abused by someone whose last name was Broom? Was her occupation housecleaning or did the broom represent witchcraft in her family line?* I wasn't sure. Eventually, after more prayer the interpretation became clear. As a small girl, Mary had become angry with her brother and had broken a broom across his back, severely injuring him. After the incident they were separated, and she was never able to ask his forgiveness. As a result, Mary had gone through life not forgiving herself for her violent act.

When the correct interpretation of this Rhema word was given to Mary, she broke down and began to weep uncontrollably. Indeed, it was true. This suppressed memory of the past was the root of her emotional problem. After recognizing it, she was immediately freed from a life of emotional imprisonment caused

142

by self-hatred. Mary was thankful for the prophetic word, but I was equally thankful for the proper interpretation. Had I given a hasty interpretation of Mary's word, she might have never received the deliverance she so desperately needed.

Application

Application is the final stage in the development of a prophecy. After distinguishing the source of your revelation and interpreting it correctly, you must then know how to apply your Rhema word. Should it be given privately to the individual or publicly for all to hear? Should it be presented in the form of poetic prophecy, exhortation, or prophetic counseling? Should your approach be straightforward or diplomatic? And, most important, do you present your revelation with grace, judgment, soberness, or humor? These are some of the questions facing the person who desires to successfully deliver a prophetic word.

Without close consideration being given to these questions, however, most people will experience undesirable results in the application of their prophecy. I have witnessed this breakdown in prophetic protocol over and over again. In fact, I have encountered scores of Christians who rightly receive and interpret revelation, but fail to apply it correctly. For example, I was in a meeting where a prophetic person singled out a young man and began to minister to him. He said, "I see a vision of a black stain on your heart, and I interpret that as sin in your life." He then proceeded to expose the young man's sins publicly, calling him to repentance.

The prophecy appeared to be an accurate word from God. However, because I knew the young man's history, I rejected the word on the basis of incorrect application. It's true, there had been moral failure in the man's life, but I knew that he had fully repented many years ago. In my opinion, the revelation of the dark stain and its interpretation was accurate but the application was dead wrong. What the young man needed was a reminder that God had already forgiven him, not another call to repentance. He needed encouragement and affirmation of God's love, not fresh condemnation and guilt from an immature prophet.

Like the prophetic person mentioned previously, we have all received a valid revelation now and then. Yet, the fact that we see a truth about someone's life, does not mean that we have the correct interpretation or application, for that revelation. Hence, we must strive to minimize our failures by growing in an understanding of the three stages of prophetic protocol — revelation, interpretation, and application. If proper emphasis is placed in these areas by those prophesying, it would greatly diminish our chances of delivering a faulty prophecy.

Conditional Prophecy

In addition to that of human error in the realm of revelation, interpretation, and application of prophecy, there is yet another twofold reason for failed prophecies. The first component relates to the will of man. The second has to do with the conditions set forth by God for a prophecy. When these factors are present, some of the most gifted prophets can encounter difficulties in the fulfillment of their prophetic word.

In light of this, we must ask the following questions. Does man's will contribute to the success or failure of a prophecy? Will God cause a prophetic word we have personally received, to come to pass without our consent? Are there spoken prophecies that never materialize because certain conditions aren't met? If so, why is this?

Before answering these questions we must first determine the latitude of man's will. To begin with, the Bible supports two basic truths. First, man has been given considerable freedom to exercise his will. Since he possesses this freedom of choice, his will is not subject to the demands of heaven or hell. He, alone, has the sole right of decision making and can utilize it for good or bad, right or wrong. Second, God does not arbitrarily violate a person's will to

144

achieve His purpose in their life. He has chosen to work within the boundaries of human will, which oftentimes, limits Him to the consent of mankind. So, when God has a purpose for a man and expresses it through prophecy, the man's will must be submitted to that prophetic purpose.

Therefore, both **the success and failure of a prophetic utterance is contingent upon the mental posture of the person receiving the word.** The person either complies with that word, denies its power, or worse, incurs judgment in their life by an act of their own will. Based on this premise, **all prophecy is conditional.**

This principle is clearly illustrated in the Book of Exodus. Initially, God spoke the prophetic word to Pharaoh, "Let my people go!" Pharaoh hardened his heart and, as a result, incurred God's judgment upon Egypt and its land, waters, buildings, produce, livestock, and people. God also spoke a prophetic word to Israel declaring that they would leave Egypt and enter a land of promise called Canaan. Instead of receiving that word and being obedient to it, Israel received the evil report that "There were giants in the land and we were grasshoppers in their sight." The generation that had been delivered from bondage in Egypt, became bound by their fears. By being disobedient to God, they incurred His wrath and died in the wilderness, never reaching their destination.

Who was to blame? Was the word which they received a true word from God? Indeed it was! God had fully revealed His intentions for Israel, through the prophet Moses. However, the children of Israel were reluctant to align their wills with the prophetic word spoken to them. Because they had set themselves against God by grumbling, complaining, and walking in unbelief, the Word of God was made null and void in their lives. As a result, the promise was passed on to the next generation. Those to whom the promise was made died without ever receiving it. At the same time, their offspring became the beneficiaries of a prophetic word that was not initially spoken to them.

Elsewhere in the Bible, we see this same principle working in reverse. According to the Book of Jonah, God had purposed the destruction of a city called Nineveh and instructed Jonah the prophet to declare this imminent judgment. Yet, after hearing the prophetic word of God, the citizens of that city humbled themselves and repented. As a result, the word spoken by the prophet didn't come to pass. Obviously, Jonah was not happy with his failed prophecy, but he learned that prophecy is conditional depending upon the posture of man's will.

Overview of Prophetic Failure

In this chapter, we covered three basic areas of prophetic failure. In the first few pages we discussed the fear of failure. Next, we talked about the need for correct revelation, interpretation and application of prophecy. Finally, we explored the conditional nature of prophecy. Let's summarize what we have learned.

First, we should never let the fear of failure neutralize our prophetic gifting. When we fail, we need to get up and try again and again until we get it right. Remember, we will not be judged for making an honest mistake. God sees us as children and makes allowances for our growth and development. (Note: As previously indicated, the trial and error method does not apply to directional or correctional prophecy. It only applies to basic prophetic ministry such as edification, exhortation, and comfort.)

Second, once becoming fluent in prophecy, we must learn how to minimize our mistakes. When we receive prophetic insight from God, we must be sure that we have the right interpretation and application for that word before we deliver it. This will increase our accuracy and bring greater credibility to our ministry.

Finally, be aware that prophecy is conditional. Since man's will is involved, there will be some prophetic words which will never come to pass. So, when giving or receiving a prophecy remember, the success of that prophecy could depend upon the recipient's compliance with the Spirit of God. **Remember, we cannot turn our backs on God nor set our wills against His purpose and expect a prophetic word to blossom in our lives.**

Chapter Twelve

PROPHETIC PITFALLS

In the previous chapter, we discussed some of the issues surrounding prophetic failure. They were: the fear of failure; the need for proper revelation, interpretation, and application; and the conditional nature of prophecy. In this chapter, we will expand upon this understanding by examining several other pitfalls related to the success and failure of the prophetic.

In the English language, pitfall is defined as *a lightly covered hole in the ground, designed to entrap unwary prey.* In a broader sense, pitfall speaks of any kind of hidden danger. When Paul writes about the "snare of the devil" in II Timothy 2:26, the Greek word *pagis* is used meaning, a trap that is set. So, in both secular and biblical language, pitfalls are places of entrapment that should be avoided at all cost.

The old gospel road is filled with dangerous pitfalls. There are opportunities to fall prey to the snares of the devil at every turn. Many who walk circumspectly will avoid these snares, having their "feet shod with the gospel of peace" (Eph. 6:15). Others who are ignorant of Satan's devices will be taken captive by him at his will. The choice is ours, we can choose to stumble in the darkness or allow the Lord to be "a lamp unto our feet, and a light unto our path" (Psa. 119:105).

What are some of these snares in relation to the prophetic? How do they damage those who prophesy? How do they limit the effectiveness of prophetic people? Once we understand the potential pitfalls of the prophetic, what action can we take to avoid them? We will answer these questions in the following pages and expose a few of the more critical pitfalls related to prophetic ministry. However, it must be understood that our goal is not to

149

discourage prophecy by promoting unnecessary fears, but to uncover the hidden traps hazardous to prophetic people.

"Thus Saith The Lord"

In today's church a "God told me" mentality seems to dominate the thinking of many believers. Just ask Christians their opinion on something and usually you will get a "God told me" or "The Lord showed me" response. It seems that God speaks to those believers hundreds of times a day, about hundreds of different things. Everything from doctrinal issues to world events fall under the umbrella of "Thus saith the Lord."

Young Christians have also learned to use these magic words to their own advantage. When their opinions are contradicted by spiritual truth or biblical logic, they will often resort to the same old "God told me so" tactic. If you continue to press them, they will eventually jump the fence of reasoning with a statement like, "Hey, all I know is what God has revealed to me!" From that moment on, all effective, two-way conversation is concluded, since one would be hard-pressed to argue with a believer who hides behind a "Thus saith the Lord."

Prophetic people also contend with a similar temptation. They, too, are tempted to declare, "Thus saith the Lord" in every situation. This is especially true of undeveloped prophets who feel under pressure to come up with a word from God. As a result of peer-pressure, they often times confuse God's voice with their own opinions. **Driven by impatience, many immature prophets are compelled to speak that which God has not said. Consequently, they give prophetic assumptions rather than divine guidance.**

Many prophetic people have had to learn this lesson the hard way. With me, it began some years ago when I was conducting a prophetic conference on the West Coast. While in the process of ministering to a group of people, I turned to a lady and boldly declared, "Thus saith the Lord." Before I could finish my prophecy

150

I was interrupted by the inner voice of God. He whispered these words to my spirit, "I am not speaking to this lady right now — you are on your own." He further indicated that I could speak for myself, but I could not use His name to make my point.

I immediately corrected myself and said to her, "Thus saith Larry." Assuming that I was making a joke, everyone began to laugh at my statement. I, too, paused and chuckled for a moment. Then to the surprise of those in the room, I proceeded to speak prophetically into the lady's life. I'm not sure how well it was received; however, in my mind, I was taking the approach that Paul used when he said to the Corinthian church, "...I say this, as my own word, not as the Lord's." He went on to say that his opinions relative to the issues addressed, were most likely the same as the Lord's: "...that is my opinion, and I believe that I, too, have the Spirit of God" (I Cor 7:12 and 40, New English Bible).

It is important to note that in this Scripture the apostle seemed to be saying, "Thus saith Paul," to the believers at Corinth. In my opinion, he was not attempting to play God, but was simply taking the liberty to express his own thoughts, as one who possessed the mind of Christ. I'm sure Paul's words were true, inspired, and packed with godly wisdom, but at the same time, he wasn't comfortable in declaring it as a *"thus saith the Lord"* statement.

Likewise, unless you are certain that God is speaking directly into a situation, it would be better to leave His name out of most prophecies. It would be safer to say "I think, I feel, I sense, I perceive, I discern, etc.," than to box yourself into a corner with a "Thus saith God." Furthermore, if you have an opinion about something, then call it an opinion or a prophetic opinion if you will, but by no means should you call it *the word of God.*

If you do involve God in something He has not initiated, the consequences could be severe. You could be judged according to the scripture found in Deu. 18:22 (RSV). ***"When a prophet speaks in the name of the Lord, if the word does not come to pass***

151

or come true, that is a word which the Lord has not spoken; the prophet has spoken it presumptuously." If you fail this test, you could be labeled as a false prophet.

King James Vernacular?

I once heard a story in Mexico that went something like this. A gringo and a Mexican were riding together in a car, arguing about the color of God. The white man insisted that God was white, the Mexican was convinced God was brown. Suddenly, the car ran off the road killing both men. Moments later they awoke in heaven in front of the Pearly Gates. As they approached God's throne, the white man began to shout with excitement. Pointing at the Great White Throne he yelled, "See, I told you God was white just like me." About this time, the Lord leaned over and said to both of them, "Hola muchachos, bienvenidos" (Spanish for "Hello, friends, come on in").

Like those men in the story, we, too, think that God looks and speaks the same way we do. Nevertheless, God, who is a Spirit, is neither white, brown, black, red, or green; nor is He bound to any one form of communication. He chooses to speak to people in their own language, not because He prefers one language over another, but for the sake of their understanding.

God is bigger than our culture or language. In light of this fact, we should never attempt to limit the Almighty to one particular people, group, or dialect. This truth is especially important for the Christian who is a devoted fan of the King James Bible. Those who live, breathe and quote this translation should be aware that The King James version is only one of the many translations taken from the original Greek and Hebrew Scriptures. Therefore, when preaching or prophesying, it is not unspiritual or unscriptural to omit some of the *yea, nay, thus*, and *thou* words characteristic of sixteenth century English (King James language). In fact, people will be more inclined to hear your message if they are addressed in a language that is familiar to their ears.

I know that I'm treading on the sacred ground of many believers. I'm also aware that I run the risk of being labeled a heretic. Nonetheless, those who are dogmatic about prophesying or preaching exclusively in King James vernacular should consider several issues.

First, the Word of God didn't originate in merry old England and Jesus didn't speak the King's English while on earth. Our Lord was not related to Robin Hood, nor did his disciples come from Sherwood Forest. He was born in the Middle East some 1600 years before the King James Bible was ever envisioned. He was also Jewish and spoke in an Arabic tongue. So, by all means read, study, memorize, and cherish the King James translation, but please don't try to convince yourself or others that it is the ultimate translation or that you must use it to get the proper results.

Second, we must try to break the King James stereotype that is common to most prophetic people. I am not suggesting that we discard the King James Bible, but when possible we should read other translations and commit the passages to memory. As a result, our preaching style and prophetic delivery might become richer and less constrained. **Remember, if it is God's word, then it can survive a diversity of translations.**

Finally, if we serve a God who is bigger than language, then we too, must not be narrow-minded in our communication. So, the next time you are tempted to prophesy in this manner -- "Thus saith the Lord God Almighty, thou art extolled by Him that sitteth upon the circle of the earth," try to restrain yourself. Instead, say something like -- "Hey, I really think that God loves you!"

Screamers

Many prophetic people have a tendency to prophesy with a loud voice. With the energy of a cattle-yard auctioneer they yell, scream, and holler at their audience. The longer they speak the louder they get, until someone responds by buying what they are

153

selling. The result is usually a hand clap from the audience, a cheer, or a barrage of amens.

This is especially true of many Pentecostals and Charismatics. There is a basic belief that the anointing is equivalent to noise. The theology is: "The louder the volume, the greater the power." By shaking the walls of the church with a high-decibel prophecy, they are convinced that God will come through with greater impact. On rare occasions this may be true, but usually screaming is nothing more than a frantic attempt to compensate for inward fears, insecurities, and a lack of authority.

There is a time to be forceful and a time to be gentle and soft. The proper approach (forceful or gentle) depends on the dynamics of the situation at the time of the prophecy. If you need to lift your voice to be heard in a large room or auditorium, then by all means speak forcefully. Or if there is a need to penetrate a dull, sleepy, atmosphere with volume, then that too, can be in order. However, in most cases, it is not appropriate to yell in peoples' faces. Such behavior is rude and can be an insult to the intelligence of those who are receiving your ministry. So, the next time you feel compelled to scream a prophecy in church, remember ...most Christians are not deaf!

Furthermore, if God does not yell nor scream at His people, neither should we. It's true that the prophets of old often, "cried out with a loud voice." However, we must understand that they yelled, not because it was the religious thing to do, but because they were addressing masses of people without the aid of a public address system. Therefore, when attempting to prophesy, find a microphone and speak to the congregation in a normal tone of voice. I assure you it will not hinder the anointing. For "It is not by might nor by power but by my Spirit saith the Lord" (Zech. 4:6).

God's Word or Human Disposition?

> "...They angered Moses at the water's of Meribah, and it went ill with Moses on their account; for they made his spirit bitter, and he spoke words that were rash" (Psa. 106:32-33, RSV).

We have been called to express God's attitude, not human mood and temperament. Moses learned this lesson the hard way. While in the desert he was told by God to strike a rock with one blow, thus creating a miraculous flow of water. Instead, he became angry with the murmuring crowd of thirsty Israelites and smote the rock twice. By displaying an improper attitude, Moses misrepresented the heart of God. As a result, he fell under divine judgment.

Like Moses, it's very common for today's prophets to speak out of their own disposition. Although they understand the dangers of misrepresenting God -- anger, strife, and bitterness often affects the purity of their prophetic word. If they have had a recent fight with their spouse, you can bet the Church will receive a scathing rebuke. If they are feeling melancholy, then a disheartening prophecy will eventually surface. Likewise, when they are experiencing a season of inner joy, the church is bound to hear about the goodness and mercy of God.

In light of this, let me make one thing absolutely clear. **The art of representing God is to do what God does, when God does it.** Therefore, prophetic people must be willing to cry when God is crying and laugh when God is laughing. However, like Moses, most of us have it backward. We often smile when God is crying or cry when God is laughing. We have not learned to lay aside our emotions long enough to express the disposition of God. As a result, the Church doesn't know whether to repent or rejoice.

For example, I was in a meeting where someone stood up and prophesied, "Thus saith the Lord, God hates your guts."

155

Immediately, half of the people in the building bowed their heads to repent of whatever it was that had made God so mad. As I looked at the person prophesying, I began to chuckle inside. I wasn't about to receive such a prophecy. To begin with, I knew that God loves his children and would never say such a thing. Next, I discerned that the person prophesying had been harboring bitterness toward other Christians. And, finally, in my estimation the prophecy had come from *hurt,* not from *heaven.* With these things in mind, I finally bowed my head and thanked God that His word is not subject to human mood.

This incident and others like it, has taught me two great truths. First, before you speak for God, make sure that your heart is a reflection of God's heart. **Last, never dress up human disposition with a "Thus saith the Lord."** If you do, like Moses, you could be severely judged for misrepresenting God.

Marriages and Babies?

There are instances in the Bible where marriages were consummated as a direct result of prophetic words. Hosea was instructed by the word of the Lord to "take unto thee a wife of whoredoms," whose name was Gomer. When Abraham's servant went out to find a wife for Isaac, he was told, "The Lord...will send His angel with thee and prosper thy way." Eventually the servant was led to Rebekah, the daughter of Bethuel. In addition, the angel of the Lord told Joseph in a dream, "Fear not to take unto thee Mary thy wife" (Hosea 1:1-2; Gen. 24:40; Matt. 1:20).

In addition to marriages, there are several instances in Scripture where children were born as the result of prophetic prediction. Occasionally their names and genders were also given before conception. The mother of Samson was told by the Angel of the Lord, "Thou art barren, and barest not: but thou shalt conceive, and bear a son." As the father of John the Baptist was serving in the temple an angel said to him, "Fear not Zacharias: for thy prayer is heard; and thy wife Elisabeth shall bear thee a son, and thou shalt call his name John." Finally, Mary was told by the Angel Gabriel, "Behold, thou shalt conceive in thy womb, and bring forth a son, and shalt call his name Jesus" (Judges 13:3, Luke 1:13, Luke 1:31).

Most predictions concerning marriages and babies in the Bible are described in the last two paragraphs. However, these incidents are the result of God speaking directly to those involved or by angelic visitation. In the cases of Samson, John, and Jesus an angel prophesied their births. In other instances concerning marriages, there was a personalized word directly received from God's Spirit. **Yet, in no instance of scripture -- other than Isaiah's prophecy concerning the birth of Jesus and John the Baptist -- are babies and marriages predicted by prophets.**

In spite of the lack of biblical support for prophesying marriages and babies, many prophetic people still continue to venture into this area of prophecy. In certain cases, the results have been devastating. Barren women who have received prophetic words of hope from "marriage and baby prophets" often slip into deep depression after failing to conceive. In other instances, infants foretold to be boys, turn out to be girls and vice versa. Most commonly, marriages that are consummated as a result of so-called "prophetic words" are often shipwrecked after years of struggling with relationships that were never meant to be.

These horror stories are a testimony to the dangers of overstepping scriptural guidelines. As previously indicated, the Bible is our manual for prophetic protocol. Therefore, as a prophetic people we must conduct our ministries in a way that is consistent with the patterns found in Scripture. **If the Bible speaks out on certain issues, then we, too, can speak with confidence. If the Bible is silent on an issue then we must exercise extreme caution**. We must take into consideration that things documented and repeated in Scripture must be of importance. Likewise, things scarcely mentioned may be of lesser significance.

Such is the case of prophesying about babies and marriages. Although it is not out of question to give such prophecies, these types of words should be more the exception than the rule. In my mind, the ratio should be something like one baby or marriage prophecy for every hundred prophecies of a different nature. And, finally, when these prophecies are given, they must be delivered with confidence and accuracy by mature and capable prophets, not with the hit and miss tactics practiced by some prophetic ministries.

Therefore, immature prophets who have overextended themselves in this area of prophecy need to be reminded of two things. First, their presumption exposes them to the danger of operating in the realm of soul power and soothsaying. **Last, there is a fine line between the divine and divination, and without the checks and balance of Scripture, anyone is capable of crossing this critical line.**

(Note: I have prophesied over barren women and have later seen God honor the prophetic word with the miracle of childbirth. At times, I have also been able to pinpoint the gender and exact date of delivery. Nonetheless, because of the recent dealings of God in my ministry, I have begun to restrain myself in this area of prophecy. For the sake of Scriptural purity and prophetic balance, I am increasingly reluctant to venture into any gray areas of prophecy, especially babies and marriage.)

Money

One of the most common pitfalls for prophetic people today is the issue of money. Predicting great wealth for others or prophesying with the motive of personal gain can be an alluring snare of the devil. For those who maintain a level of prophetic integrity, this may not be an issue. Yet, **Like Balaam of the Old Testament, many latter-day prophets have become** *prophets for* _**profit.**_ In other words, they are prophets to the church only if it profits them first (Jude 11).

In many instances, high-dollar prophets have cheapened their ministries with unholy tactics (selling their gifts for gain). While some of these prophets blatantly beg for money, others peddle tons of religious paraphernalia and gospel trinkets. Everything from 1-900-Dial a Prophet Network to $100 prophecy lines, holy water, healing oils, and anointed clothes have been marketed and sold under the guise of advancing the kingdom of God.

As a result, this sort of nonsense has diminished the value of the prophetic and, in due time, those who have merchandised themselves and their gifts in this fashion will be exposed. They will be marked by God as having "...forsaken the right way, and are gone astray, following the way of Balaam the son of Bosor, who loved the wages of unrighteousness" (II Peter 2:15).

The Bible clearly teaches that "The laborer is worthy of his reward." It is also true that; "Those who minister should be counted worthy of double honor." Yet, when there is a season of financial leanness, we should <u>never</u> resort to prophetic manipulation for money. In spite of our lack, we must possess the same kind of integrity that motivated Elisha the Prophet to refuse excessive gifts from Naaman the Syrian. Elisha realized that God's free expression of love for Naaman, as evidenced by God healing him of leprosy, did not entitle the prophet to take advantage of the Syrian's great wealth (I Tim. 5:17-18, II Kings 5:1-27).

Like the prophet Elisha, we too, must declare that **the Word of the Lord is not for sale. Freely we have received, freely we should give.** Anything less is a direct violation of true spiritual ministry and will be met with the wrath of God's judgment.

Just as Jesus overturned the tables of merchandise in the Temple and drove out the moneychangers, He shall also appear in His righteous wrath and judge those who would fleece His flock today. With whip in hand, He will purge His Father's temple from the flea-market mentality of buying and selling the things of God. That which has become a "den of thieves" will be cleansed and restored to a house of prayer and free ministry. As a result, we, as ministers, will learn to give expecting nothing in return. Like God's priest who served in the Old Testament Temple, we will seek no inheritance other than the richness of God's Spirit.

(Please understand, I am not suggesting that prophetic ministries refuse honorariums and offerings for their labor. Neither am I saying that they should refuse love gifts from those whom they have encouraged in the Lord. What I am saying is, "material gain cannot be a priority." **Money must never take precedence over ministry. Neither should the lack of it dictate how much you minister, nor to whom you minister to.**)

Prophetic Manipulation

Webster's Dictionary defines manipulation as follows: "To control the will or emotions of another person by exploiting feelings such as guilt or affection to one's own ends; shrewd or devious effort to manage or influence for one's own purposes; to appropriate or control by skilled use."

The most serious pitfall awaiting those who minister in the prophetic is the temptation to manipulate people and circumstances with the gift of prophecy. Prophetic people who are rich in emotion and abundantly gifted can readily arouse people's interests and stir their hearts. Due to their capacity to hear from God, they serve as powerful magnets, drawing to themselves those who thirst for a word from God. As a result, they quickly win accolades and favor making it easy to manipulate most believers.

This stands in direct opposition to the purpose of the prophetic. After all, **prophetic ministers are called to support and confirm the will of God in people's lives, not to manipulate**

160

them. They are also instructed in the Bible to encourage the Church, not to control it.

In spite of this truth, I have observed ministries that have greatly abused the Church and manipulated God's people in three different areas. First, there are prophets who have used their gifts to extort large sums of money from unsuspecting Christians by declaring, "God says give all to the prophet of God." Second, others have used their giftedness and charisma to gain influence, manipulate leaders, and control circumstances that are favorable to their position. Finally, the most dangerous manipulators are those who influence the opposite sex to act in ways that are immoral and unbecoming.

Some of these ministers have prophesied that believers should divorce their marriage partners and find their true soul mates. Others have suggested that women become intimate with them as an act of servanthood, assuring them that it is all right to indulge in a lifestyle of promiscuity. Much like the prophet Balaam they "...cast a stumbling block before the children of God," causing weak Christians to commit fornication (Rev. 2:14).

How do these prophetic ministries manage to gain such power over peoples' lives? To begin with, their persuasive personalities serve as a hook to ensnare those of lesser maturity. Subsequently, because the essence of prophetic ministry revolves around the power of words, everything spoken by prophets has a dramatic impact on the hearers. **<u>Like a guided missile, the words of a prophet can seek out a target of weak conscience or guilt and explode deep within the soul of that person</u>**. Even those things spoken in jest or casual conversation can penetrate the most guarded heart and bring the person under the influence of the prophet's intentions. For that reason, in view of the power of prophetic words, prophets should exercise extreme caution in the manner with which they conduct their lives and ministries.

161

Finally, prophetic people should keep a guard on their mouths at all times and recognize that every word spoken has the potential to wreak devastation. They must realize that every word which leaves their mouth will take root and produce seed after its own kind, either good or bad. **Prophets have the ability to either bless or curse with their mouths**. Jesus said,

"And I will give unto thee the keys of the kingdom of heaven; and whatsoever thou shalt bind on earth shall be bound in heaven: and whatsoever thou shalt loose on earth shall be loosed in heaven" (Matt. 16:19, emphasis mine).

Counterfeits

That which God initiates, Lucifer attempts to duplicate. This dynamic can be seen in every aspect of Christian experience. Any time a real work of the Holy Spirit takes place, rest assured that the devil will attempt to replicate it with a counterfeit. This principle also applies to the prophetic.

For example, when the Holy Spirit imparts prophetic revelation to the Church, Satan is also at hand, ready to inject a counterfeit anointing. This counterfeit gifting can come in many forms. It can surface as blatant Satanism, white magic, palmistry, channeling, crystal healing -- or it may appear as the seemingly harmless New Age movement.

Those who are ignorant of Satan's devices, often fall prey to one or more of these pitfalls. **However, all spiritual activity which exists outside the parameters of God's Word and the Holy Spirit is false and will incur judgment.** It is absolutely forbidden by God in Scripture and addressed in this manner: "There shall not be found among you anyone...that uses divination, or an observer of times, or an enchanter, or a witch, or a charmer, or a consulter with familiar spirits, or a wizard, or a necromancer. For all that do these things are an abomination unto the Lord" (Deut. 18:10-12).

A few years ago this truth was made real to me in a very personal way. I had been touring the nation, ministering in various churches and conferences. On one occasion I was in Phoenix, Arizona, conducting a prophetic conference for a group of churches. While en route to the meeting, I heard a familiar sound coming from a side room in the lobby. It seemed to be the voice of a man prophesying. Simultaneously, there was the sound of a weeping female (whom I assumed was the recipient of prophetic ministry). Apparently her cries were the result of a prophetic word relating to her past. She was given accurate information, such as dates and specific details concerning childhood trauma and then exhorted to release the past and move on with her life. With great delight I stepped out of the lobby and into the room, hoping to witness the ministry of the Holy Spirit.

However, as I leaned over and peeked through the partially open door, I was stunned. Much to my surprise, there were tables filled with crystals and chairs occupied by New Agers. It was apparent that I had stumbled onto a New Age seminar, where the power of physic perception was being demonstrated.

How can this be true? Has the world capitalized on counterfeit giftings? And are they experiencing results? Yes, in fact, they not only possess a form of prophetic perception, but excel in its use. From television psychics who can tell you your mother's name, to fortunetellers who can accurately predict your child's future, this generation is filled with false ministers who are quick to demonstrate their psychic powers. Nevertheless, no matter how spiritual these things appear to be -- **fortune-telling, seances, secret covens, Ouija boards, psychic phenomena, New Age spiritualism, etc. -- are pitfalls which reek with the odor of false anointing and must be avoided at all cost.**

163

Chapter Thirteen

PROPHETIC WEIRDNESS

One of the most disturbing snares related to the prophetic is the exhibition of *weirdness*. Due to the bizarre behavior and strange mannerisms of a number of prophetic people, the world has developed preconceived ideas about the prophetic which are incorrect. For example, when the word *prophet* is mentioned, two distinct images appear within the minds of both sinner and saint. These images are *weird* and *bizarre*. Although the words weird and bizarre bear close resemblance, each group — sinners and saints — views them in a different manner, and for the most part both are wrong.

To most Christians, the stereotype of a prophet is one who is bizarre, archaic in thinking, crude in manners, and caustic in attitude. They are seen as hermits or cave dwellers who occasionally crawl out of their most holy habitations to rebuke a worldly church. When they appear on the scene, a paralyzing fear strikes the hearts of both man and beast. Dogs begin to howl, babies cry, and women scramble for shelter, hiding their children from the wrath of these spiritual godzillas!

As these giants ascend to the hallowed heights of the pulpit, hell and earth fall silent awaiting their commands. Everyone is breathless, knowing that a single move of the prophet's hand can topple empires, set churches in order, and expose the sins of carnal believers. No one is exempt; even demons flee from the lightning bolts that issue from the end of their long bony fingers. Although these prophets are called to the ministry of *equipping* the saints they usually end up *whipping* the saints. Wielding giant clubs, these Neanderthals show up at the church ready to administer a beating. Ruthlessly, they rip the hide off the backs of both sheep and shepherd and then pour salt into their open wounds.

165

After thoroughly persecuting the saints, these prehistoric prophets mount their steeds, return to their Stone Age strongholds and go into holy hibernation. Finally, after a season of strange visions and weird dreams they rise once again, put on their camel hair coats, eat a bowl of gun powder, pick their teeth with grasshopper legs and prepare to minister again. <u>This is the picture most Christians have concerning the prophet and his ministry.</u>

In contrast, the world has quite a different perception of the prophetic. Instead of the medieval mentality held by the Church, the secular view of the prophetic is one of New Age imagery, closely resembling the *Star Wars* and *Star Trek* movies. To them, a prophet is more of a "prophetic space cadet" than a normal man. He is a universal guru of sorts who has ascended to the spiritual heights of the third heaven. Going where no man has gone before, his intergalactic ministry reaches out to regions unknown where he is able to contact and communicate with spiritual entities of extraterrestrial origins.

In addition, he is a kind of new age superman, able to leap tall buildings in a single bound. He flies by astro-projection, communicates with the dead, reads minds, and sees through the obscure. With the help of his crystal ball and the strength of his psychic powers, he sets the pace for a whole new breed of spiritualist. For this sort of space prophet the Spirit of God is simply the force within. Satan is just an illusion from the dark side. Speaking in tongues is merely an eastern chant. Being slain in the Spirit means entering a state of unconsciousness through transcendental meditation. Prophesying is a form of crystal gazing. And waiting on God means that the prophet is so spiritually advanced that he must slow down and wait for God to catch up with him. <u>This is the mind-set of the world concerning prophetic ministry.</u>

Both views in this chapter, religious and worldly, serve only as reminders of the extreme misconceptions and myths that face prophetic people. Due to these false concepts there are few people

166

who perceive prophetic ministry as being a normal, rational expression of Christian experience. Their negative perception of the prophetic is enhanced, not only by these myths but by prophets who conduct their ministries in a weird or unusual fashion.

Weird or Strange?

To the average observer there is little difference between weird and strange. Yet, to those who are alert and spiritually in tune, the two words are actually quite distinct. While weird denotes being odd, queer, and bizarre; the word strange is defined as unusual, extraordinary, and peculiar. The first is closely akin to eccentric behavior, which is unnatural and unacceptable. The latter relates to uniqueness and is an acceptable biblical expression.

I have encountered both weird and strange prophets. While some of these prophets exhibit moderation, others seem to be much more pathetic than prophetic. At first, they may appear to be spiritual, but weird prophets are usually bizarre, spooky, and spiritually imbalanced. They profess to be pure as snow, but in most instances they can be more brainless than sinless. Driven by an ego larger than life, they humiliate not only themselves but others who embrace their theatrical antics.

May God save us from this kind of present-day weirdness. It's true that we are often seen as being a strange and peculiar people, but that doesn't mean we have to act in a weird fashion. Like our biblical counterparts, we have the right to be unusual in our manner and method of ministry but, we must also be user-friendly to the general public. I agree that we are called to be different, but we are not called to be bizarre.

Therefore, I have a few things to say to weird Christians: **Knock it off! Stop trying to be super-spiritual and just be yourself! Quit imitating others!** You are not called to be another Elijah or John the Baptist, nor are you a prophetic parrot. You are just you; unique in personality, diverse in style, and different in

167

expression. So, relax and **learn to be supernaturally natural**. Drop the weird stuff, and maybe God will entrust you with a legitimate ministry, one that is real and refreshing.

Bizarre Prophecies

One of the byproducts of prophetic weirdness is bizarre prophecy. If a prophetic person is eccentric and unnatural you can be assured that most of their prophecies are also off the wall. This person might be able to hide it for awhile, but sooner or later the foolishness of his heart will be expressed in his actions and with his lips. "For out of the abundance of the heart his mouth speaks" (Luke 6:45, RSV).

Over the years, I have witnessed much of the craziness that is generated by weird prophets and bizarre prophecies. I have seen a number of self-proclaimed seers, who are convinced that their weirdness comes from God. In obedience to the so-called *Word of the Lord*, they have filled the gas tank of their stalled car with sugar, thrown rocks through the walls of the church sanctuary, handcuffed themselves to the pews of the church, and have bound and gagged members of their congregation with duct tape.

Others have prophesied the end of the world within 24 hours, the instantaneous melting of snow on Mt. Ararat (which will supposedly reveal the location of Noah's Ark), and the formula for making hair spray. They have declared that the Antichrist would emerge from the headquarters of the Democratic party, that the Church would take over the world by military force and that God was sick in bed, unable to perform His duties.

In one instance, a prophetic person stood up and said: "Thus saith the Lord God, I have seen your despair, yea, I know how you have suffered with your sickness, yea, I am also aware of your struggle with depression and suicidal thoughts, yea, I understand, for I, the Lord went through the exact same thing last week." On another occasion someone prophesied the following: "Yea, saith

168

the Lord, I was going to speak to you but I forgot what I was going to say, so please pray for my memory, saith the Lord." In another church, a lady stood up and declared, "Thus saith God, just as Abraham parted the Red Sea, I shall also part your troubled waters." She sat down slowly, pondered the prophecy for a minute, stood up again and said. "Thus saith God, I have made a terrible mistake, it was not Abraham but Moses who parted the Red sea."

Judging Weird Prophecies

"Let the prophets speak two or three, and let the others judge" (I Cor. 14:29).

Due to some of the crazy things said and done in the name of prophecy, it is necessary for believers to judge all things. Yet, other than the Bible and personal discernment, there seems to be no universal yardstick which we can use to systematically measure or judge prophecy. In each instance when prophecy is given, we must take into consideration all the dynamics present at the time. **When judging prophecies, we must make allowance for the mistakes of immature people.** We need to extend grace and mercy to all prophetic words given by beginners and release them from any undue sense of condemnation or heavy-handed judgment. On the other hand, we must not be tolerant of the crazy and bizarre prophecies uttered by weird Christians.

There are times when weird prophecies are given by perfectly normal people. Many times these prophecies are the result of fear, nervousness, or inexperience. Usually, they are innocent mistakes made through ignorance or a slip of the tongue. In light of this, it would be unwise to judge these people harshly or correct them publicly. All that is needed is a little back room instruction and a lot of encouragement. With proper training and instruction, these Christians can be groomed to operate with a clear, concise, gift of prophecy.

169

In contrast, there are other prophetic people who are deliberately bizarre. Unlike the beginner, these Christians are more neurotic than nervous. As previously stated, they are just plain weird and must be dealt with firmly and openly. If they exhibit weirdness in a church meeting, they must be addressed and challenged publicly. If they refuse this correction, they must be marked as being rebellious and without discipline.

Therefore, in all instances where weirdness is displayed, correction must follow. However, it is not always necessary to correct weird people in a harsh manner. Sometimes you can apply the proper correction by employing clever or humorous tactics. These tactics can be just as effective as a severe rebuke and, if applied correctly, can take the sharp edge off of a strained atmosphere. Ultimately you get the same results minus the mess created by a cold, calculated rebuke.

A good example of correction through humor was told to me a few years ago. It all began in a particular church where prophetic ministry was both taught and encouraged. It seemed that in every meeting three or four people would stand up to give a word of prophecy. In spite of warnings from the pastor concerning wayward prophecies, there was always someone who would speak a word that made absolutely no sense. Not wanting to discourage those who possessed a legitimate gift of prophecy, the leaders chose to tolerate this weirdness for a season of time. They hoped that things would eventually get better.

Consequently, when their hopes diminished and patience failed, the elders called a meeting to initiate a plan of action. The plan was simple. The next time someone gave a weird prophecy it would be addressed immediately. They prayed that God would give them a creative way to neutralize the weirdness without bringing offense to others who were truly prophetic.

The following week, someone stood up in their next meeting and began to prophesy. In a mystical tone of voice this person declared, "Thus saith the Lord: I have placed a table before you. I have put a plate on the table and a hammer on the plate. Yea, there is also a fork on the table and a spider crawling on the tablecloth." A hush fell over the church. With great expectation, everyone sat on the edge of their seats awaiting the interpretation of the prophecy. *What could it mean? they mused. Did the plate represent God's provision? Was the hammer a type of the word? Was the spider the devil? And what about the fork? Did it speak of communion or warfare?* No one was really sure.

Finally, one of the elders who was present in the previous meeting, slowly stood to his feet and approached the microphone. With a grin on his face he said, "This is the interpretation of the prophecy. Take the hammer and break the plate. Take the fork and kill the spider. Turn the table over and, by all means, rebuke the person who gave this prophecy."

Needless to say, that was the end of prophetic weirdness in that particular church. The next time an opportunity was made for prophecy, people were a bit more careful with their words. They knew that if they were to give a weird prophecy it would be met by an even weirder interpretation. As for the leaders of the church, they had learned to fight fire with fire.

User-Friendly Prophetic

Prophetic weirdness is usually symptomatic of a much deeper problem. **Oftentimes, people who act weirdly, do so because they have a false concept of spirituality.** The real root of this problem is embedded in the belief that being spiritual means being unreal, unnatural, and inhuman. Since they have not learned to be *naturally supernatural*, they are prone to express a fake spirituality with bizarre behavior. As a result, they and their ministries are not compatible or user-friendly to the church.

There are several other misconceptions that can prevent believers from being user-friendly. One of these, is the idea that

171

we are called to be *deep*. Many Christians equate this so-called spiritual depth with obscure utterances, mystical revelations, and hard-to-understand visions. In fact, a few of these believers are so deep that they make absolutely no sense to anyone but themselves. As one sarcastic preacher said, "We have become so deep that even God has trouble understanding us."

Why have we shrouded our ministries with heavy revelations, abstract analogies, and deep sayings? Why do we feel we have to act deep and mystical in order to appear spiritual? The answer is clear. We have departed from the simplicity which is found in Christ. In an attempt to impress people, we have taken the simple things of God and made them hard to understand. We have not learned that, **the art of true spiritual ministry is the ability to take complex issues and make them simple.**

By way of illustration, the ministry of Jesus was characterized by His ability to decode spiritual mysteries. He constantly converted the deep things of God into teaching that was understandable to the masses. He made His ministry user-friendly with the use of parables and stories about fishing, farming, etc. Although He possessed a great depth of understanding, He knew that in order to reach simple men, He must speak on their level.

As His disciples, we would be wise to follow our Lord's method of ministry. If we want to connect with the common person, then we must come down from our spiritual high horses and meet the people where they live. Like our Master, we must be approachable, and our ministries must be accessible and down-to-earth. **We must try to keep it simple, speaking the language of life as opposed to the language of religion.** Otherwise, we will never be able to relate prophetically to a generation that is looking for user-friendly churches and ministries.

172

User-Friendly Principles

No two ministries are exactly the same in style and method. We are all unique in personality and distinct in our expression of God. As believers, we see things and do things differently. Yet, in spite of this diversity, there are a number of basic guidelines which can be applied to all who operate in the prophetic. The following is a list of these user-friendly principles:

(1) Speak audibly. For the sake of others don't whisper or mumble.

(2) Don't scream -- neither God nor His church is deaf!

(3) Avoid speaking swiftly. Fast talkers are hard to understand.

(4) Don't be lengthy. When you ramble on, people lose interest.

(5) Don't repeat someone else's word. Redundancy is not always confirmation.

(6) Speak in harmony with the atmosphere of the meeting. Don't contradict the flow of the Holy Spirit.

(7) Beware of speaking harsh judgment or condemnation. Always try to encourage!

(8) Don't monopolize a meeting. Give others a chance!

(9) Keep it simple. Don't try to be deep or mystical!

(10) Stick to the point. Don't try to cover too many issues.

(11) Don't mimic others. Be yourself!

(12) Be direct. Avoid mystical illustrations when possible.

(13) Avoid disruptive mannerisms. Don't be theatrical.

(14) Speak calmly. Don't hype the audience.

(15) Develop your own speaking style. Avoid exclusive use of King James Vernacular.

(16) Don't speak from anger, hurt, etc. Only speak the mind of the Lord.

(17) Don't come across as super spiritual. Haughtiness will limit your effectiveness.

(18) Speak with humility. Remember pride comes before a fall.

(19) Don't speak first if you are a novice. Let those who are mature set the pace.

(20) Be willing to have your words tested. You are not beyond error.

Concluding Thoughts

In this chapter, we have placed a heavy emphasis on the negative aspect of prophetic weirdness. We determined that bizarre prophecies, although laughable at times, can be counter-productive to the growth and development of our prophetic ministries and must be confronted and corrected whenever possible. The exhortation to prophesy simply and in a normal fashion was also underscored by developing several user-friendly guidelines. The purpose of these principles was to help curtail the sometimes dangerous effects of prophetic weirdness.

Nevertheless, I must admit that it is one thing to critique a problem and another to offer a workable solution. If this be the case, then, what is the solution for prophetic weirdness? The answer is obvious, we need to grow up in Christ. We need to let go of our tendencies toward prophetic weirdness, and begin to embrace normalcy.

For example, in the same way that a child overcomes his childish idiosyncrasies by growing up into maturity, we can overcome our abnormal behavior by growing up in Christ. Like the Apostle Paul, we will reach a place of growth were we can declare, "When I was a child, I talked like a child, I thought like a child, I reasoned like a child. When I became a man, I put childish ways behind me" (I Cor. 13:11, NIV).

In view of this truth, spiritual maturity serves as the primary antidote for much of the weirdness that surrounds immature prophetic people. Therefore, in the next chapter we will examine some of the issues relating to maturity. First, we will establish maturity as a deterrent to weird behavior. Last, we will see how maturity plays an essential role in the proper administration of the prophetic.

Chapter Fourteen

PROPHETIC MATURITY

Christian maturity denotes a state of being where one is complete in God, thoroughly developed, and fully grown. It reflects being responsible beyond duty, bearing the burdens of others, giving more than you receive, loving more than you are loved, going the extra mile with your brother, endeavoring to keep the unity of the Spirit, and esteeming others better than yourself.

In I Cor 13:11 (RSV), maturity is characterized by the words of a great apostle who declared, "When I was a child, I spoke like a child, I thought like a child, I reasoned like a child; when I became a man I gave up childish ways." The implication of this verse is that we, as Christians, are called to exchange a lifestyle of immaturity for one of maturity. As a result, pride is replaced with purity, ignorance with wisdom, lust with love, selfishness with selflessness, and impatience with patience. This is the essence of spiritual maturation.

Indeed, maturity is the obvious goal for every Christian. Yet we must understand that maturity does not come to us overnight. **We are not born mature, nor at any point in life do we receive the gift of instant maturity. On the contrary, maturity is developed over a period of time. It is a process wherein we develop "...precept upon precept, line upon line."** And, in this process of development, we are privileged to grow up in Christ, "...being changed into the same image from glory to glory, even as by the Spirit of the Lord." For some, this can happen in a matter of years, for others it could take a lifetime (Isa. 28:10, II Cor. 3:18).

We only need to look at the world around us to illustrate this point. For instance, everything in God's world matures in one fashion or another. Whether it be plants, animals, trees or people,

177

all of creation begins in infancy and reaches forward to a degree of perfection. The lion is born small and helpless, hardly able to see or walk. But through a process of growth, the lion becomes a strong, majestic animal often referred to as the *king of the beasts*. Likewise, a tree begins as an insignificant little seed but eventually matures to the point where it's capable of producing fruit and shade.

The same is true of Christian maturity. In Isaiah 61:3, we as believers, are referred to as being "...trees of righteousness, the planting of the Lord." In Psalm 80:15, David refers to the Church as God's vineyard. Jesus also declared in John 15:5, "I am the vine, ye are the branches. He that abideth in Me and I in him, the same bringeth forth much fruit."

Like the tree and the vine, we must also submit to God's growth process. We must learn to tolerate the uncertainties associated with Christian development, weather the storms of life, and endure the harsh realities of spiritual winters. To survive this process we must sink our roots deep into the soil of God's kingdom and commit ourselves to the process of "abiding in the vine." As a result, we will grow strong in the Lord, develop Christian character, and bear an abundance of fruit.

Yet, herein lies the problem. In keeping with the theme of this chapter, how many prophetic people are willing to begin their ministry in small and insignificant ways? How many budding prophets have the heart to endure the discomforts and humiliation brought about through the painful process of development? During this time of maturation, can we, who are prophetic, learn to conduct our ministries in a way that is not harmful to the church? Can we minister in a season of immaturity while learning to be mature? If so, then what area of growth do we give our attention to? What kind of childishness must we put away, and to what degree must we embrace maturity? In the following paragraphs we will discuss these questions.

Charisma or Character?

Christians who aspire to operate in prophetic ministry should learn three important facts. First, your gift does not make you mature. Second, your measure of spiritual gifting should not exceed your measure of spiritual fruit. Finally, **charisma is never an adequate substitute for character.**

These three truths are clearly seen in Paul's exhortation to the Corinthian church. As a spiritual father, the apostle praised the believers for their knowledge and gifting by saying, "In every way you are enriched in Him with all speech and all knowledge..., so that you are not lacking in any spiritual gift" (I Cor. 1:5-7 RSV).

Yet two chapters later his compliment seems to fade into the severity of a stinging rebuke. He states, "But I, brethren, could not address you as spiritual men, but as men of the flesh, as babes in Christ...for you are still of the flesh. For while there is jealousy and strife [immaturity] among you, are you not of the flesh, and behaving like ordinary men?" (I Cor. 3:1-3, RSV).

What is being implied in Paul's exhortation? Was he double-minded in his evaluation of the Corinthian church? Was he confused or possibly demented? Of course not — he was only drawing attention to the dichotomy which existed within the lives of these early believers. The Corinthians excelled in the nine gifts of the Spirit such as tongues, interpretation of tongues, prophecy, etc. However, they were lacking in the development and expression of the nine fruits of the Spirit — especially, long-suffering, gentleness, kindness and meekness.

Much like the Corinthians, we are also, "ever learning and never able to come to the knowledge of the truth." **The present day Church is filled with believers who possess Bible knowledge and spiritual gifts, but are devoid of Christian character.** Many of these contemporary Christians are able to preach, prophesy, perform miracles, and heal the sick; however, because their gift greatly exceeds their fruit, their lives and ministries are in jeopardy. When they stand before Jesus on Judgment Day they will ask the question, "'Lord, Lord, did we not prophesy in Your name, and cast out demons in Your name, and do many mighty works in Your name?' The Lord will answer, 'I never knew you. Depart from Me, ye evil doers'" (II Tim. 3:7, Matthew 7:22, RSV).

In light of this, the Lord is raising up a new breed of prophetic people. These prophets will be more concerned about character than charisma. They will never allow their gift to outshine their fruit. Nor will they confuse talent with maturity. Most important, **integrity will outlive inspiration and their intimacy with Christ will exceed their ministry in the Church.**

Possessing Maturity

It's one thing to confess maturity and yet another thing to possess it. For example, a child may declare that he is an adult a thousand times a day, but until he actually grows up, he convinces no one but himself. Regardless of his relentless confession, reality dictates that he is still a child in every sense of the word. On the other hand, when the child does reach maturity, there is no longer a need to boast about it. Everyone knows he is an adult, not because he says so, but because he looks and acts like an adult. In essence, he has become that which he has confessed.

Jesus said in Matthew 12:33 (RSV), "...the tree is known by its fruit." In other words, a tree is defined by what it produces, not the name given to it. For example, you can plant a tree in your backyard and tell your neighbors that you now have an apple tree. However, if the tree doesn't produce apples, all the words in the world will not convince them that it's a real apple tree. Yet, if the tree bears apples, you will not have to make a single statement about the nature of the tree. Your neighbors will know it is an apple tree, not because you declare it, but because the fruit speaks for itself.

180

The same is true of prophetic maturity today. **It's is not what you say but what you are that makes the real difference.** If you truly are a seasoned prophet, then you won't have to confess it to the Church. It is not necessary to wear a neon sign around your neck declaring your office, nor will is it beneficial to hand out business cards introducing yourself as "God's Prophet." All that's required is the works of a prophet and the fruit that follows. By simply being what God has called you to be, the Church will recognize your prophetic office and respond to it.

What a wonderful thought. **If you have to convince people that you are a prophet, you have most likely demonstrated that you are not a prophet.** For example, Jesus, who was the greatest prophet of all time, functioned as a prophet to the Nation of Israel. Yet when it came to titles He merely referred to Himself as the *Son of Man*. His desire to be known as the Father's son seemed to be more important than bearing the title *prophet*. Consequently, it was left to others to recognize and proclaim His prophetic office. Such was the case in John 4:19 when the Samaritan woman said to Him, "Sir, I perceive that thou art a prophet."

Timing

"...who then is the faithful and wise steward, whom his master will set over his household, to give them their portion of food at the proper time?" (Luke 12:42, RSV).

Another crucial issue of prophetic maturity is timing. Proper timing is absolutely essential for the delivery of a prophetic word. If your timing is right, you can integrate fresh revelation into peoples' lives with little difficulty. **Like water falling on dry ground, a word in season has the potential to refresh the spiritual landscape of the Body of Christ.** On the other hand, if your timing is wrong, you may encounter problems in the delivery of the most basic prophetic word.

For instance, truth out of season is like a musical note out of sequence. A single, solitary musical note may sound beautiful when played by itself. However, if the note is presented at the wrong time, it can be disruptive to the harmony and to the flow of a song. Likewise, a word of prophecy may be valid and pure within itself, but counterproductive when spoken out of season.

Consequently, it isn't good enough to receive and arbitrarily speak prophetic truth. Just because a word is true doesn't mean that a person is spiritually ready to receive it. On the contrary, we who are prophetic must learn to deliver truth in the right sequence at the right time. As a result, we will not be found guilty of creating undue stress and discomfort for those who are incapable of handling truth out of season. Like the wise steward in Luke 12:42, we will know when "...to give them their portion of food at the proper time." For, "a word spoken in due season, how good it is" (Proverbs 15:23).

To better illustrate this truth, I want to draw an example from personal experience. Some years ago, I was asked to minister to a group of upcoming leaders in a particular church. Before I began, the pastor of that church requested that one of his young men, who was prophetic, minister alongside me. The pastor explained that he had a desire to expose the young man to a different flow of prophetic ministry. I agreed and briefly instructed my new partner about the basics of prophetic protocol. Shortly afterward, we began to prophesy over those who were designated to receive ministry. Everything was fine until we came to a gentleman we will call Bill.

When I began to focus on Bill, I perceived he had a high calling upon his life. I immediately saw the enormous potential of his ministry and the spiritual gifts which God desired to give him. At the same time I was also aware of his immaturity in the areas of pride and self-promotion. In light of this, the Holy Spirit impressed me that any kind of revelation concerning this man's future ministry, no matter how true, could be counterproductive to the present work of God in his life.

The Spirit continued to instruct me that my prophetic perception about the potential of Bill's ministry was accurate, but the timing for such a word was premature. So I simply prayed for the gentleman and started to move on to the next person. About this time, the young man who was assisting me turned to Bill and began to prophesy the exact same thing that the Holy Spirit had restricted me from saying. The young man clearly detailed Bill's calling and future ministry, holding nothing back.

Needless to say, everyone in the room was excited about the prophecy. Bill was elated beyond words and the young man who gave the prophecy was now beaming with delight. Nevertheless, I was saddened by the negative implications of a right word which had been spoken out of season. Knowing what God had shown me about Bill's character, I was sure that the fulfillment of his calling had been jeopardized by a premature prophecy. Bill would probably spend the rest of his life wrestling with spiritual pride. Truth out of season would become his enemy, not his friend.

Was the young man mistaken about the prophecy he gave? Did he misinterpret the purpose of God for Bill's life? No, I believe God had truly called Bill to a spectacular ministry. Yet the revelation of his calling should have been kept secret until such time that Bill could have humbly received it. It's true the young man had tapped into a prophetic vein of truth, but, by telling Bill everything he saw, he was more of a hindrance than a help. He made the mistake of applying knowledge without wisdom.

Watchman Nee, in his book *The Spiritual Man, Volume I* (pg. 162-163), addressed this problem of tell-it-all ministry. He clearly describes the actions of believers who are unable to keep their mouths shut. Although he targets Christians in general, the following can also apply to those who flow in prophetic ministry. He begins by saying:

Some Christians who are indeed soulish find special delight in helping others. Since they have not yet reached maturity, they do not know how to give food at the proper time. This does not mean these do not have knowledge; actually, they have too much. Upon discovering any improper element or when told of some difficulty, they immediately assume the role of senior believer, eager to help with what limited insight they have. They pour forth scriptural teachings and experiences of saints in lavish abundance. They are inclined to tell all they know, nay, perhaps more than they know, now reaching into the realm of supposition. These "senior" believers exhibit, one after another, everything which has been stored in their minds, without at all inquiring whether those to whom they speak really have such a need or can absorb so much teaching in one session. They are like Hezekiah who opened all his storehouses and showed off all his treasures.

I believe Watchman Nee was right. Therefore, in context with his writings, please remember two things. First, **spiritual maturity is not defined by what you know, but by what you do with the knowledge you have.** Second, concerning prophecy in a specific sense, it is often a greater act of maturity to remain silent than to speak a word out of season.

In relation to this truth, I once heard Paul Cain say, **"a prophet is known on earth by what he sees and says, while a prophet is known in heaven by what he sees and doesn't say."** What an incredible thought! If this is true then believers who hear from God must learn to keep certain things to themselves. They must keep a guard on their lips at all times, speaking only that which is permitted by God. Otherwise, the Lord will not trust them with secrets relating to people and their problems.

Compassion

One of the most crucial aspects of prophetic ministry is compassion. Without this godly attribute, a prophet is nothing more than an indifferent oracle, methodically speaking forth correction, direction, judgment, etc. — without concern for the

184

feelings of others. Like a computer, he can spit out information that he has received. However, he is incapable of applying it with discretion, or in a manner that is appropriate to the need at hand. He coldly pronounces and denounces, without feeling responsible for the consequences of his word. Furthermore, his failure to develop a mature love for the church often prompts him to speak corrective words rather than words of consolation.

On the other hand, the prophet who truly possesses godly compassion will always attempt to season his words with grace, hope, and kindness. As one who commands the prophetic office, he has the right to rebuke and correct the people of God, but he will use this privilege only as a last resort, not as a first response. This prophet's goal is not to malign the Church by passing judgment, but to defend it through prayer and intercession, in hope of restraining the wrath of God. When God does give him an irreversible word of judgment, like Jeremiah the weeping prophet, he will not deliver the prophecy until it has been thoroughly bathed in his own tears.

Compelled by compassion, the mercy prophet will always choose hope over hopelessness, intercession over destruction, and mercy over judgment. His compassion for God's people will drive him to the prayer closet before he enters the pulpit. In an attempt to intercede for those who are subject to the wrath of God, he will wrestle with the Almighty, relentlessly and unashamedly.

Moses, a Mercy Prophet

In the Bible, there are numerous examples in which mature prophets are characterized by their compassion and mercy. Although these prophets were often called upon to declare divine judgment, their compassion for the church seemed to exceed their desire to condemn the church. We find an example of this in the Book of Exodus were we see the prophet Moses contending with

God in behalf of the children of Israel. In the Living Bible, Exodus 32:9-14 records the event as follows:

> Then the Lord said, "I have seen what a stubborn, rebellious lot these people are. Now, let Me alone and my anger shall blaze out against them and destroy them all. And, I will make you, Moses, into a great nation instead of them." But Moses begged God not to do it. "Lord, he pleaded, why is Your anger so hot...turn back from Your fierce wrath. Turn away from this terrible evil You are planning against Your people! Remember Your promise to Your servants" So, the Lord changed His mind and spared them.

This account illustrates how God confronted Moses with a decision to show either judgment or mercy to Israel in the wilderness. Perhaps divine judgment was fitting for such a rebellious people, but instead of agreeing with the execution of that judgment, Moses contended with God in an attempt to change His mind. As a result, God heeded the intercession of the prophet and spared the people from certain death.

Like Moses, we who are prophetic must attempt to function in a higher realm of prophetic ministry than that of rebuke and judgment. Without exception, **our protocol for ministry should be priest first, prophet second**. And, in the event that we are commanded to speak forth judgment, we must first understand God's dealings with His people. Namely, that God pronounces judgment, then looks for a man to stand in the gap as a priest to intercede against the execution of that judgment. Therefore, it is incumbent upon those who speak forth God's judgment to pronounce this judgment with their heart set upon interceding against it like Moses did.

186

Final Conclusion

As we come to the close of this book there are several points critical to the issue of prophetic maturity. First, prophetic maturity embodies much more than dreams, visions, deep revelations, the ability to prophesy, and the privilege of discerning and judging the Body of Christ. These things may be necessary for the equipping of the saints, but cannot compare to the value of comfort, encouragement, compassionate intercession, etc. So, as priest-prophet we must endeavor "...to comfort all that mourn in Zion, to give unto them beauty for ashes, the oil of joy for mourning..." (Isa. 61:2-3).

Second, we can either whip the saints or equip the saints with the gift of prophecy. We can tear down or build up, encourage or discourage. Most important, we can spend our spiritual gift to buy self-acclaim and popularity, or we can spend our lives as a token of love and intercession for the Church. Whatever the choice, remember, **we are not true prophets of God until we can first profit God's kingdom.**

Finally, the real test of prophetic ministry doesn't lie in the greatness of our spiritual gift, but in the quality of our spirit. For example, a pure heart is equal in kingdom value to that of a pure gift or theology. Likewise, in God's eyes, the condition of our heart is just as important as the condition of our ministry. It's true we are exhorted to "desire spiritual gifts," however, **we can be the greatest prophet on earth, but without love we are nothing more than sounding brass or, a tinkling cymbal** (I Cor. 13:1).

187

Appendix

FORTY COMMONLY ASKED QUESTIONS
AND ANSWERS

1. What is the gift of prophecy?

Prophecy is one of the nine gifts of the Spirit outlined in I Cor., chapter 12. Paul further states in this book that "...one who prophesies speaks to men for edification and exhortation and consolation...one who prophesies edifies the church" (1 Cor. 14:3-4).

Strong's Exhaustive Concordance defines prophecy, prophesy and prophesying as "predicting or foretelling events; to divine; to speak under inspiration; an inspired speaker; a poet." In *Scribner's Dictionary of the Bible*, W. T. Davison, describing prophecy, states that "The Hebrew word nabi, which is used over 300 times in the Old Testament, was long associated with a root word meaning 'bubble up'" (page 757). This concept of bubbling up presents a word picture that conveys an essential truth about prophecy: namely, that prophecy often springs forth or bubbles up out of the resident anointing that lies within every New Testament believer.

2. Is prophecy biblical?

The Bible is a collection of written prophecies. From Genesis to Revelation, every word is bathed with prophetic implications. The Bible also declares, "...The testimony of Jesus is the Spirit of Prophecy" (Rev. 19:10). Furthermore, since the words prophecy, prophesy, and prophesied are used over 160 times in the Bible, it is not surprising that the Apostle Paul instructed us to "...desire spiritual gifts, but rather that ye may prophesy" (I Cor. 14:1).

189

3. Is prophecy for today?

The Scripture declares that Jesus is the same yesterday, today and forever and that the gifts and callings of God are without repentance (Heb. 13:8, Rom. 11:29). Therefore, our Lord is unwavering in His commitment to endow us with spiritual gifts. If he gave prophecy to the New Testament Church, then we, too, can expect to receive and flow in the same gift. Peter establishes this truth in Acts 2:17 by declaring, "...In the last days, saith God, I will pour out of my Spirit upon all flesh; and *your sons and your daughters shall prophesy."*

4. The Bible states that prophecy shall cease. When shall this be?

Paul teaches us in I Cor. 13:8-10, "Whether there be prophecies, they shall fail; whether there be tongues, they shall cease; whether there be knowledge, it shall vanish away. For we know in part, and *we prophecy in part.* But, when that which is perfect is come, then that which is in part shall be done away."

According to these Scriptures, prophecy will vanish at the coming of that which is perfect. Many Bible teachers are convinced that this has already happened. They argue that the canonization of Scripture, which resulted in our Bible, was the perfect revelation that replaces our need for further prophecy. However, if this holds true, then according to I Cor. 13:8 both tongues and knowledge would also have passed away centuries ago. Since we know that this premise is false, one can only assume that Paul was referring to the second coming of Jesus. Indeed, our Savior is the Perfect One, and once He returns to Earth He will obviously overshadow all tongues, knowledge and prophecy. Until then, however, Scripture exhorts us to actively use the prophetic gift to build up His Bride, the Church.

5. Should the one who prophesies be a Bible teacher or theologian?

God does not prize ignorance. The right type of biblical training <u>can</u> add to and enrich one's prophetic gift. On the other hand, some highly educated believers are often lifted up in the pride of their learning and lean upon their intellect rather than the inspiration of the Holy Spirit. Due to this error, God often uses the weak to confound the wise. He also reveals His mind to babes and hides it from the proud.

6. Is the only purpose of prophecy to foretell the future?

The gift of prophecy may speak of the past, present, or future. It is also used to speak words of exhortation, edification, and comfort. For example, the prophet Samuel could look into the future and speak of things which were yet to come. On the other hand, king Saul also prophesied under the inspiration of the Holy Spirit, but the Bible doesn't record any instance where he foretold the future. Likewise, in the New Testament, Jesus, John the Revelator, Agabus, and the Apostle Paul all foretold future events. However, the Corinthian church was exhorted by Paul to prophesy edification, exhortation, and comfort. These are forms of prophecy that are seemingly without a predictive element.

7. Who can prophesy?

In I Cor. 12:11, Paul teaches that the Holy Spirit distributes the gifts of the Spirit to every man "...severally as He will." He later encourages the whole Church to "...desire spiritual gifts, but rather that ye may prophesy." Therefore, the gift of prophecy may not initially be given to all but is available to all those who earnestly desire it. This is true for both sheep and shepherd, educated and uneducated, immature and mature, male and female, child and adult. Consequently, all who have a heart to encourage the Church may prophesy.

191

8. Should prophecy be spoken in the first, second, or third person?

The point of view from which prophecy should be spoken is optional. It can either be first, second, or third person, depending upon the choice of the person speaking. For example:

a. First Person: "I am merciful, saith the Lord."

b. Second Person: "The Lord is merciful."

c. Third Person: "The Lord says He is merciful."

9. Should one stand when prophesying?

There are no absolute rules as to whether one should sit or stand when prophesying. However, if others are sitting in a meeting, you may want to stand up to indicate that the Spirit is upon you and that you are looking for permission to speak. Nevertheless, we must remember that it is the anointing which qualifies your gift, not your style, personality, or body language.

10. Should Scripture be quoted when prophesying?

Prophecy should always complement Scripture and in no instance be contrary to it. Therefore, it's beneficial to memorize, recall, and express the Scriptures that support what is being prophesied. However, it isn't necessary for all prophetic words to be couched in Scripture. It's also important to remember that merely quoting Scripture isn't synonymous with prophecy.

11. Is it right to pray for and covet the gift of prophecy?

In I Cor. 14:1, Paul exhorts us to "desire spiritual gifts, but rather that ye may prophesy." In verse 31, Paul teaches that "...ye may all prophesy." In verse 39, we are also told to covet (desire, be jealous for) prophecy. Nevertheless, our pursuit of prophecy must be founded on a right motive. We must covet prophecy for the edification, encouragement, and comfort of the Church.

12. Is the gift of prophecy greater than the gift of tongues?

Paul writes in I Cor. 14:5 "...greater is he that prophesieth, than he that speaketh in tongues." This order of priority is significant in two ways. First, Paul declares that a prophetic utterance is greater in usefulness than that of an utterance of tongues. For example, a person who is suicidal would benefit more from a prophetic word spoken to them in their own language, than from an unintelligible utterance in an unknown tongue. Second, prophecy is given for the edification of others, whereas tongues is given for building up the person giving it. Therefore, if we believe that it is more blessed to give than to receive, then we must recognize that the use of prophesy in a public setting is greater than the use of tongues, unless there is an interpretation of the message of tongues.

13. Is prophecy the greatest gift?

Although prophecy plays a prominent role in Scripture, the gift of prophecy does not excel in usefulness over all the other gifts. In fact, the greatest gift is the one which meets the greatest need at the moment. For instance, a person dying of a dread disease would benefit more from someone who has the gift of healing than from one who has the gift of prophecy (except when the gift of prophecy is used to complement the gift of healing and heighten a person's faith in God's power to heal him).

14. Should prophetic words ever be written and delivered in written form?

The greater part of Scripture is prophecy in written form. Many of the Old Testament prophets and some of the New Testament prophets recorded their prophecies which were saved for future generations. Therefore, it can be beneficial to write out a prophecy even if we intend to give it orally. An additional benefit for putting one's prophecies into writing is that once we have it in written form, we can do research and compare it to Scripture. This enables us to search for any hidden symbolism it might have to receive a more complete grasp of its meaning.

15. Should prophecy be given in the presence of unbelievers?

Although some disagree, Scripture places no limits on where to prophesy. In the Old Testament, Saul prophesied in the open. Eldad and Medad also prophesied in the camp (Num. 11:26). In the New Testament, Paul indicates that unbelievers would fall on their face and confess their sins when prophecy is uttered in a church meeting (I Cor. 14:24-25).

16. Do I deliver a prophetic word immediately after receiving it?

Proper timing is essential to the delivery and effectiveness of a prophetic word. Therefore, upon receiving a prophetic word, dream, or vision from God, it isn't always necessary to immediately release it. We need to pray over our revelation for further clarification, for faith to accurately deliver the word, and for the reception and cooperation of the person receiving the prophecy. Remember, the spirit of the prophet is subject to the prophet. This means we have control over our own spirits which enables us to withhold or release what God gives to us.

17. Is it proper for more than one person to prophesy in a church service?

Paul taught the Corinthian church to prophesy in order, one person at a time (I Cor. 14:31). The purpose of this instruction was to limit the confusion in church meetings. He taught that although two or more may sense the same anointing, have the same message, and feel motivated to speak, only one should prophesy at a time. The others should listen and then judge the validity of the prophecy.

18. Is it wise for a pastor to appoint only one person within the congregation to prophesy?

Although the Bible strongly encourages all Christians to prophesy, there are certain people who excel in the use of the gift of prophecy. Therefore, when a pastor recognizes an advanced gift of prophecy operating in a believer, he might be more inclined to place a higher degree of trust in the validity of their prophetic insight. As a result, he may be more inclined to honor their prophetic gifting and make frequent use of it. Although this is not necessarily wrong, pastors must also learn how to receive from believers who are less proficient in this gifting.

19. Can the exercise of the gift of prophecy be stifled in a church service?

The writer of I Thess. 5:19-20 warns us to "...quench not the Spirit" and to "...despise not prophesying." In light of these scriptural warnings, it's apparent that the spirit of prophesy is subject to the atmosphere created by believers. Where there is faith, desire, and respect for prophecy, the Spirit will respond by releasing prophetic expressions which emanate from the heart of God. Where there is doubt, unbelief, and animosity toward the prophetic, prophecy will be limited if not completely quenched.

For "Jesus said unto them, 'a prophet is not without honor, but in his own country, and among his own kin, and in his own house.' And he could there do no mighty work, save that he laid hands upon a few sick folk, and healed them" (Mark 6:4-5).

20. If a pastor stops me from prophesying in his church when I feel I have a word from God, would I be in disobedience to God if I submit to the pastor's wishes?

You're not sinning by cooperating with or submitting to the authority God has placed over an assembly of believers. If the pastor is wrong in rejecting your ministry, God will deal with him. If the pastor is sincere in his heart but mistaken about you and your gifting, God will bless him anyway and eventually teach him to better discern the Body of Christ. In the meantime, God won't require you to interrupt or take over his service. So, remember, it's always better to submit to godly authority than to undermine it.

21. How does one begin to receive prophetic words from God?

All Christians are unique in personality, nature, and spirit. Therefore, none of us receives or hears from God in exactly the same way. While some hear the audible voice of the Lord, others receive an inward witness of the Spirit in their hearts. Some have dreams, while others see visions. Some have Scriptures quickened to their minds, while others receive mental pictures. A number of believers feel different sensations in their body, such as burning, shaking, etc. Others feel nothing more than a keen sense of awareness which emerges out of the depths of their spirits.

22. Can people who have a valid gift of prophecy make a mistake and continue to grow in their gifting without being labeled a false prophet?

As New Testament believers, we have been given the latitude to prophetically express the heart of God in our own words. Accordingly, when one is prophesying, one's temperament, personality, doctrinal ideas, and level of maturity play a vital role in the delivery of prophecy. Therefore, mistakes can be made if the speaker fails to properly interpret the mind of the Spirit. Also, one's nervousness or inexperience add to this margin of error. The apostle Paul states, "For we know in part and prophesy in part," and "...prophesy one by one that all may learn" (I Cor. 13:9, 14:31). This supports the proposition that we can grow in our prophetic gifting and still have the freedom to learn from our mistakes. However, the mistakes made arise from the speaker, not from the gift. People make mistakes whereas God cannot err.

23. Will God punish people who prophesy out of their own spirit?

If a Christian is sincere in his heart but immature in his gifting and doesn't know how to yield or appropriate the anointing, God will bear with him for a season until he refines his gift. For example, if your child was hungry and asked you for food in a wrong way or with a poor attitude, would you punish him or let him starve? Of course not! You would feed the child in spite of his speech or approach. The same is true of prophecy. God is neither quick to judge or punish us for our mistakes or immaturity.

24. Are all dreams prophetic in nature?

Not all dreams convey a real message to the dreamer. Solomon teaches us in Ecc. 5:3 that a number of dreams "...cometh through the multitude of business..." On the other hand, there are times when dreams carry a specific message from God. These dreams are supernaturally inspired and should be carefully interpreted and applied in our lives. Most of the recorded instances of God speaking to man in the Bible are through dreams and visions. Job states, "In a dream, in a vision of the night, when deep sleep falleth upon man, in the slumberings upon the bed; Then he [God] openeth the ears of man and sealeth their instruction..." (Job 4:13).

25. Is prophecy given exclusively for the benefit of believers?

Scripture indicates that the basic purpose of prophecy is for the edification, exhortation, and comfort of the Church. However, there are instances in the Bible where prophecy was given to unbelievers. In one instance, a prophetic dream from God was given to the Pharaoh of Egypt. As a result, Joseph interpreted the dream (having already interpreted the prophetic dreams of Pharaoh's butler and baker). He was then elevated into the second highest position in Egypt so that he might deliver Israel and the Egyptians and the surrounding countries from severe famine and drought. In another place in Scripture, it is recorded that the Chaldean king Nebuchadnezzar was also given prophetic dreams. A prophet called Daniel interpreted these dreams which ultimately lead the king to declare, "Now I Nebuchadnezzar praise and extol and honor the king of Heaven..." (Gen. 41:1-50 and Dan. 4:37). Consequently, both of these dreams served as tools of evangelism and salvation for the world.

26. How do I know that the word I received is from God?

Jesus declared in John 10:4 that his sheep "...know his voice." Although mature sheep often hear and recognize their master's voice, that doesn't mean that little lambs are familiar with the Great Shepherd's voice. Therefore, until we are mature enough to rightly discern and identify the voice of our Master, we must test all things that we hear and see. We must not only judge the revelation that we receive but also test the spirit behind the revelation.

27. How are we to judge prophecy?

I Thess. 5:21 instructs us to "prove all things; hold fast that which is good." Paul declares, "But he that is spiritual judgeth all things..." (I Cor. 2:15). To the Corinthian church he writes, "Let the prophets speak two or three, and let the others judge" (I Cor. 14:29). Therefore, it isn't an option to judge prophecy, but a commandment. However, we must not confuse criticism with righteous judgment. Our purpose for judging prophecy is to discern and separate truth from untruth, and spirit from flesh — not to critique the mannerism, method, and personality of the person, which often bleeds through prophetic utterances. In fact, Scripture teaches us that we are to test the spirit, not the mannerisms of the person prophesying (I John 4:1).

28. Is there a particular style or method one should use when prophesying?

There is no set standard, method, mannerism, nor behavior required when prophesying. While some Christians choose to speak loudly and forcefully, others are comfortable speaking in a normal tone of voice. Just as some people are demonstrative by nature, others are more subdued. Whatever the case may be, it's important to reflect upon the words of John the Baptist who said, "He must increase, but I must decrease" (John 3:30). Like John, we must not draw too much attention to ourselves when moving in the prophetic. Instead, our purpose must be to exalt the Lord and to encourage the brethren. Remember, whatever your style, God places His emphasis upon your character and the purity of your word — not upon your personality!

29. Can a person prophesy without the anointing of the Holy Spirit?

There are times when well-meaning Christians give a prophecy without the inspiration of the Holy Spirit. However, we cannot say that they are sinning by doing so. Due to an overzealous spirit, some of these believers are inclined to overstep the maturity level of their gifting and, as a result, speak out of their human spirit, imagination, or intellect.

30. Can I have the gift of prophecy and not know it?

The Bible often portrays God as a farmer who plants seeds in hopes of reaping a mature crop at a later time. The same is true of the gift of prophecy and other spiritual gifts. Many times these gifts are imparted to us in seed or embryonic form. As a result, they often lie dormant within our spirit, hidden for an extended period of time beneath the conscious level of our soul. Therefore, we must learn to identify, cultivate, and nurture the gifts given to us and to those whom God has given us influence over. We must learn to see those things that are not as though they are.

31. Is it possible to have the gift of prophecy and not have love?

Love is a fruit of the Spirit that comes out of godly character. In contrast, prophecy is a gift of the Spirit given to us by the Holy Spirit, independent of our ability to love. Therefore, Christians may be enriched in knowledge and laden with spiritual gifts, but not possess the love of God. Such was the case of the believers in Corinth. Paul sharply rebuked these first century believers for their error. In I Cor. 13, he declared love to be the greatest gift of all. He further indicated that mature believers are characterized by the expression of their gifting through love.

32. Are there different levels of prophetic ministry?

There are four basic levels of prophetic utterance and ministry. The first pertains to the Spirit of prophecy and is a corporate anointing. It falls upon a gathering of believers enabling those who are not prophets, or those who don't possess the gift of prophecy, to prophesy.

The second level relates to the gift of prophecy and is a resident endowment of the Spirit given to certain believers at the discretion of the Holy Spirit. The third level incorporates a prophetic mantle and is a ministry function empowered by a strong prophetic anointing that rests upon an individual at all times. The fourth level is the office of prophet, which is a governmental position mentioned in Eph. 4:11. This is a fivefold ministry function given to the Church for the purpose of foretelling, rebuking, affirming, bringing revelation, encouragement, direction, and ministry confirmation.

33. If I prophesy, does that mean I am a prophet?

Sawing a board or hammering a nail now and then doesn't make one a carpenter. Neither do we become a professional race car driver just because we know how to drive an automobile. One is a lifelong profession requiring commitment, skill, extensive training, dedication, discipline, etc. The other is an occasional activity, secondary to your life's purpose. This same principle also applies to the prophetic. The fact that you can prophesy, or that you possess the gift of prophecy, doesn't necessarily qualify you for the office of prophet.

34. If I make a mistake in prophesying does that make me a false prophet?

If a policeman is involved in a case of mistaken identity and arrests the wrong person, does that mean he is a false policeman? Likewise, if a pastor makes a mistake in counseling one of his flock, does that make him a false shepherd? Of course not! We are all imperfect people and make mistakes now and then. Therefore, the difference between false and true prophets doesn't always lie in the perfection or accuracy of their prophetic words but in the attitude or motive of their hearts. For example, a false prophet can be accurate in what he says, but wrong in his heart and spirit. On the other hand, a godly prophet can be mistaken in his prophecy but pure in his heart. Which of these do you think God will honor and endorse?

35. Other than speaking prophecy, are there other forms of prophetic expression?

Song, dance, drama, mime, etc. have all been used as vehicles of prophetic expression. For instance, the Book of Psalms is a collection of prophetic songs. In the Book of Exodus, we see Miriam, the sister of Moses, leading the women of Israel in a prophetic song and dance. In addition, the Song of Solomon, which some consider to be one of the most prophetic books in the Bible, was written as a play. Finally, many Old Testament prophets, such as Jeremiah and Ezekiel, acted out their prophecies much like a mime would silently act out a story.

36. Is prophecy conditional?

Man has been created in the image of God and has been given a free will. As a result, man possesses the freedom of choice. In light of this, God is reluctant to violate our will in order to bring His purposes to pass in our lives. Therefore, the success and failure of a prophetic utterance spoken over us is contingent upon the will and mental posture of the person receiving the word. By choice, the person either complies with the word, denies its power, or worse, incurs judgment in this life. For example, in the Old Testament Israel received a prophetic word that they would enter into Canaan, the land of promise. However, since they set their heart against God's word by murmuring and complaining in disobedience, they incurred God's wrath and died in the wilderness, never reaching their destination.

37. Is it ever proper to speak correction and rebuke through prophecy?

The primary purpose of the New Testament gift of prophecy is to bring edification, exhortation, and comfort to the Church. Yet, there are times when it is necessary to prophesy correction and rebuke. Nevertheless, this should come as a last resort, not as a first response. Furthermore, using the prophetic to bring a corrective word or a rebuke is reserved solely for those who operate out of the governmental office of a prophet.

38. Can I give direction for believers' lives through a prophetic utterance?

Directional prophecy is a dynamic which is better served by those who minister in the office of a prophet. Occasionally, there are instances when God will use prophetic believers to give words of direction, such as where to move, where to work, etc. However, this is more of an exception than the rule. So, before you prophesy direction, remember, God will hold you responsible for sending His children down the wrong path in life.

39. What are the gifts of the word of knowledge and the word of wisdom? How do they relate to the gift of prophecy?

The word of knowledge is one of the nine gifts of the Spirit outlined in I Cor. Chapter 12. It's the supernatural ability to discern and speak forth things known to others, but, at the time, not known to you. For instance, when this gift operates through believers, they know certain things about total strangers, both past and present. Many times this knowledge includes a *specific word* about vocations, sicknesses, family problems, financial status, names, birthdates, etc. This does not reveal new information to the one receiving ministry. However, his faith and level of expectancy is heightened by hearing a complete stranger identify specific details about his life.

The gift of the word of wisdom is also one of the nine gifts of the Spirit. It's also a supernatural ability used to discern and speak forth God-breathed wisdom for a particular person or situation. For example, those who exercise this gift often speak into peoples' lives concerning God's wisdom for their future. In many instances, revelation is given to guide individuals as to how and where they are to conduct their lives, and with what timing.

The word of knowledge and the word of wisdom are complementary to the gift of prophecy. These gifts seem to flow together in one prophetic stream, making it hard to distinguish one from another. However, there are different characteristics inherent to these gifts. Whereas the gift of knowledge and the gift of wisdom are narrow in scope of revelation, the gift of prophecy is panoramic in scope and vision. For instance, a word of knowledge is one word relating to a specific detail, either past or present. The word of wisdom is one word which reveals God's plan and wisdom for the believer's life. In contrast, the gift of prophecy brings to light numerous details concerning the past, present, and future. When exercised, prophecy releases information, inspiration, encouragement, conviction, correction, judgment, etc. Unlike the word of knowledge and wisdom, it is given for the benefit of the corporate Church as opposed to that of one believer. Most important, it is the testimony of Jesus Christ (Rev. 19:10)

40. How do I learn to hear God's voice?

God, who is divinely unique has also made us unique. Therefore, it is difficult to teach others how to hear from a God who is diverse in expression. Depending on the circumstances God speaks in many different forms, ranging from an audible voice to an inner voice, from dreams to visions, and mental pictures to inner impressions. Yet, in spite of how we hear from God, we can become more receptive to His voice and attentive to His ways through prayer, fasting, meditation, worship and intense scrutiny of the Scripture. Therefore, to enhance our ability to hear God's voice, we must begin to commune with God on a daily basis.

To obtain a list of other resources (books, tapes, & videos) on the prophetic, including instruction upon how God may grant prophetic insight and revelation to those called into business and assist them in their fulfillment of His purposes within the realm of commerce; Or, to obtain additional copies of this book, please contact:

Cherith Publications
1925 Century Park East, Suite 2130
Century City, Ca 90067
(800) 555-1359 or (310) 475-8761
Fax (310) 475-2781

Thank You!

To invite Larry Randolph to speak to your group or for a list of tapes and videos, please address your correspondence to:

Larry Randolph Ministries
1925 Century Park East, Suite 2130
Century City, Ca 90067
Fax (310) 475-2781

Order Form

Please send **User-Friendly Prophecy** to:

Name _____

Address _____

State_____ **Zip** _____ **Phone** _____

Enclosed is my check for _____ copy (s).

Each copy is $12.95 plus $3.00 tax & shipping. Please make your check payable to **Cherith Publications**. Then, please send it to 1925 Century Park East Suite 2130 Century City, CA 90067.

To **Fax** your order dial **(310) 475-2781**.

Charge to my MC   Visa   Exp. Date _____

Card Number _____

Signature _____

Phone us your order @ **(800) 555-1359**

Thank you!